MASS MEDIA AND RURAL DEVELOPMENT

About the Author

Arbind K. Sinha is known among young anthropologists for his constant advocacy of the use of cultural understanding for the betterment of mankind. He was involved in action research projects among the tribals of Chhotanagpur, Bihar.

Sinha entered the field of communication, with an anthropological background, with the start of the Satellite Instructional Television Experiment. That was the beginning of his career in Communication Anthropology. Organiser of sessions in the Xth International Congress of Anthropological and Ethnological Sciences, New Delhi and the XIth Congress in Canada, Sinha worked on projects which aimed at the societal use of satellite communication programmes. He has also established himself in the field of disaster warning.

For a while, Sinha was deputed to work with the Government of Gujarat to take appropriate technology to the rural areas of Gujarat State. He is presently working as a scientist in Space Applications Centre-ISRO, Ahmedabad and is engaged in a number of satellite based communication projects. He is also on the faculty for the training of the INSAT television programme production personnel. warning.

Mass Media and Rural Development

A Study of Village Communication in Bihar

Arbind K Sinha

CONCEPT PUBLISHING COMPANY PVT. LTD.
NEW DELHI-110059

ISBN: 978-81-7022-094-7

Edition 2025

Published and Printed by

Concept
Since 1974

Concept Publishing Company Pvt. Ltd.
A/15-16, Commercial Block, Mohan Garden,
New Delhi-110059 (India)
T: 91-11-41101460
E: publishing@conceptpub.com, *W*: www.conceptpub.com

ACKNOWLEDGEMENT

IT was the beginning of 1974 when I joined the Satellite Instructional Television Experiment (SITE) Social Evaluation Project of the Space Applications Centre, Ahmedabad. This gave me a chance to do research in rural Bihar and an opportunity to learn something about the social aspects of communication. Subsequently, I was granted permission to use part of the SITE data for use in my research. I owe a great deal to the Centre and its staff for several other facilities.

I express my grateful thanks to Dr. Binod C. Agrawal, Project Leader of the above mentioned Social Evaluation Project. He extended all cooperation, gave freely of his time, and was always there whenever I needed help with ideas, suggestions, and criticism.

I do not find words for the encouragement I got from Professor Yash Pal, the then Director of Space Applications Centre, who not only visited me in the field, but was also a continuous source of inspiration. Professor E.V. Chitnis, the present Director of the Centre, who was Programme Manager, SITE, also deserves my gratitude for the benefit I have derived through his participation in workshops, seminars, and discussions on the subject.

To Professors L.P. Vidyarthi, Sachchidananda, K.S. Mathur; Doctors K.K. Verma, J.K. Doshi, Vinayshil Gautam, V.S. Upadhyay, Mangananand Jha, Onkar Prasad, Shri R.B. Lal, Shri Bageshwar Singh, and Mr N. Sudhakar Rao, I express my thanks for stimulating discussions, critical reviews, comments, and suggestions in respect of the work presented here.

Numerous inhabitants of Ismailpur—among them, one in particular, Shri Shyamnandan—need special thanks whose generous cooperation was essential to the completion of my fieldwork.

Smt. Alice Joshy helped in typing various drafts of this work and Shri K.K. Raghavan finally brought it to the present form; my thanks are due to them for their very friendly cooperation.

Last, but not the least, I extend my sincere thanks to Professor Kumudini Deo and Dr M.L. Gupta of Vikram University for their hospitality, help and cooperation.

ARBIND K. SINHA

CONTENTS

LIST OF TABLES

LIST OF PLATES AND FIGURES

PLATES

FIGURES

1

INTRODUCTION

THE DEVELOPMENTAL role of mass media is well established. Highlighting its contribution Schramm says that :

> It is hardly possible to imagine national, economic and social development going on at its present pace without some modern information multiplier, and indeed, without mass communication, probably the great freedom movements and national stirrings of the last few decades never would have come about at all (Schramm 1964 : 271).

According to Dube (1976 : 107) it plays a direct and useful role in the areas of community development movement with several communication strategies, using traditional channels and idioms as well as mass media. Though the culturally in-built communications also contribute towards development, it is such a slow area and a situation specific process that a developing country like India cannot afford to wait. India has to reach to the level, where it can provide food, clothing, and shelter to each individual, within the shortest possible time. Thus, it has become necessary to gear up the developmental process in India, where almost 80 per cent of the population lives in rural areas isolated from the urban centres and have low rates of literacy.

On the basis of past experiences, it was thought that the problem could be solved by disseminating developmental messages through agents working with the government and non-government units, print and mass media. Nascimento suggested that without effective communication, deliberately planned, organised, and directed in manner and form peculiarly relevant to the existing environment, very little in developmental terms is likely to be achieved (Nascimento 1977).

Mass media is a one-way communication from *one* to *many* ; such as newspaper, magazine, film, radio, and television. These permit a message from a source to reach a large and often widely dispersed audience. In the Indian context, Sharma and Singh (1972) indicated that mass media alone could enter the calculus of development and offer the greatest possibilities for effective action through its capability of disseminating technical expertise and useful knowledge among millions of villagers, particularly cultivators living in far-flung areas. Bogart holds the opinion that the mass media have brought the members of diverse societies into a common universe of discourse and have been an increasingly powerful force for the international unification of ideas and values (Bogart 1966 : 80).

Among the various mass media, the film and television are considered the most effective, combining the audio and visual together. To Gross, television has changed the role of mass media by making non-face-to-face communication as practical and efficient in many cases as face-to-face relation (Gross 1973 : 289).

Keeping the above views in mind, the present study attempts at understanding : (a) the role and relevance of the mass media with special reference to television, and (b) face-to-face communication as its role is considered to be greater in the rural than in the urban setting.

In India, the film remained confined mostly to urban areas and field publicity units were not found on village roads. Television was a gift of technological advancement and was introduced with the aim of providing developmental information as well as 'healthy' entertainment to the viewers.

HISTORY OF TELEVISION IN INDIA

The feasibility of television in India was first discussed in a Unesco meeting in late 1956, and the Experimental Television Service was introduced in September 1959. It started with 20 television sets in and around Delhi. Telecast was twice a week for an hour, having social education as its central theme along with entertainment. From August 1961 a new programme, the educational television service was introduced for Delhi schools. It was reorganized in 1965 and became a daily community and school programme. Later on, in early 1967, a bi-weekly programme, "Krishi Darshan" was introduced for promoting better agricultural practices among the cultivators of Delhi and the neighbouring states. More than eighty community viewing television sets were distributed and tele-clubs were organized as a part of a follow-up programme.

Till 1975, India had seven television centres at Delhi, Bombay, Srinagar, Amritsar, Calcutta, Madras, and Lucknow and a relay centre at Poona. Satellite Instructional Television Experiment (SITE) commenced from August 1975 to July 1976 (details given in the following pages). After SITE was over, the original SITE clusters were covered with terrestrial television system with relay centres at Cuttack, Gulbarga, Hyderabad, Jaipur, Muzaffarpur, and Raipur within a period of two years. Of course, the Pij (Ahmedabad) transmitter continued to work even after SITE.

Thus, till the mid-seventies, like other developed countries the television services remained confined to the capital cities and their vicinity in India. Schramm (1964) reports that in almost all countries the media cluster in the cities. Kearl has reported that "media are generally urban centred" (Kearl 1976 : 168). Chitnis (1976) finds terrestrial systems urban-bound in the absence of extensive wide-band microwave or cable network. Shroff (1976) writes that the AIR-TV (now Doordarshan) programme of India was directed towards urban school children and based on a common curriculum. Verghese (1980), Adivi Reddy (1980), and Gokhale (1979) also hold similar opinions. The main beneficiaries of television are thus, the viewers of major cities and towns. This bias could widen the information gap between urban and rural population. To Shummo, it would encourage the rural population to migrate to towns, to seek this and other privileges the town people enjoy, thereby causing environmental inconveniences and other social problems (Shummo 1977 : 29).

One of the reasons for television remaining urban centred, as cited earlier, was technical limitation of the terrestrial transmission system which could cover only up to a radius of 50 to 80 km. The use of satellite brought a revolution in the field of communication systems and this made it possible to bring the people from remote corners, face-to-face with a new reality.

The planners of India then thought of using the satellite television system to accelerate rural development by telecasting developmental messages directly to remote villages.

SATELLITE INSTRUCTIONAL TELEVISION EXPERIMENT

India's Satellite Instructional Television Experiment or SITE, as it is popularly known, was a vision of the late Vikram A. Sarabhai. He was of the opinion that :

> in any developing country, one of the prime ingredients of development is the dissemination of information : information about new fertilizers, seeds, insecticides, cropping patterns, and so on. The process of education is basically related to an information dissemination/transfer process. For the rapid and sustained growth of developing countries, the urgent need to disseminate information to the masses is obvious. Mass media are clearly the main component in this system of information transfer. . . . Television is ideal as a medium to convey information and news to the masses of population, on whom such an audio-visual medium would have profound impact (Sarabhai 1969 : 5).

As a first step towards this scientific experiment of international cooperation, Sarabhai, on behalf of the Department of Atomic Energy (DAE), Government of India, signed an agreement with the National Aeronautics and Space Administration (NASA), USA on 18 September 1969 known as the "Indo-US ITV Satellite Experiment Project". According to the agreement, NASA provided Applications Technology Satellite-6 (ATS-6) for one year. India took care of the designing and manufacture of ground segments, installation of television sets in the villages, their maintenance, management, programme production, and the transmission of television programmes. Some of the transmission components were given by the United Nations Development Programme (UNDP) as aid. India accelerated SITE-related activities from 1973 and NASA launched ATS-6 into space on 30 May 1974. The actual experiment (SITE) commenced on 1 August 1975 for a period of one year.

That one year SITE was conducted in 2,330 villages of six states, referred to as clusters. These states were Andhra Pradesh, Bihar, Karnataka, Madhya Pradesh, Orissa, and Rajasthan. Apart from these, 504 conventional television sets were installed in 335 villages of Kheda district, Gujarat. The districts and number of villages selected in the Bihar cluster are given in Table 1.1.

TABLE 1.1 : **Distribution of SITE villages in Bihar cluster ; districts and maintenance/sub-maintenance centres**

*Districts**	*No. of villages*	*Maintenance/Sub Centres*	*TV Sets Catered*	*Cluster Total*
Muzaffarpur	139	Muzuffarpur**	110	393
Champaran	89	Motihari	91	
Darbhanga	132	Darbhanga	80	
Saharsa	33	Samastipur	79	
		Saharsa	33	

* For the purpose of SITE, pre-1971 districts were used. However, 3 old districts were divided into a number of new districts. Muzaffarpur, district (old) is divided into three districts ; Muzaffarpur, Vaishali and Sitamarhi. Similarly, Champaran district (old) is divided into East and West Champaran (Bettiah) districts, and Darbhanga district (old) is divided into Darbhanga, Samastipur, and Madhubani districts.

** Cluster headquarters

The scope of the total experiment can be described under three sub-heads : (1) programme production, (2) transmission of programmes, and (3) maintenance of television sets.

Programme production

All the programmes for SITE were produced by the then AIR TV's (now Doordarshan) three Base Production Units in Cuttack, Delhi, and Hyderabad. In addition, science education programmes for children were produced by Space Applications Centre, Ahmedabad and Bombay SITE studios. Half-hour national programmes covering news and other programmes of common interest (partly live) were televised from Delhi. General instructional programmes on agriculture, animal husbandry, family planning, health and nutrition, and recreational programmes like myth-dramatizations, music, song and dance, and puppet shows were telecast from Ahmedabad. The recreational programmes also contained some instructional messages.

Transmission of programmes

Specially pre-recorded television programmes were telecast from Ahmedabad Television Studio. The studio was connected with the Experimental Satellite Communication Earth Station (ESCES) situated near the studio, from where the television signals were sent to ATS-6 located 35,680 kilometers, 35° south-west in outer space (*see* figure 1.1).

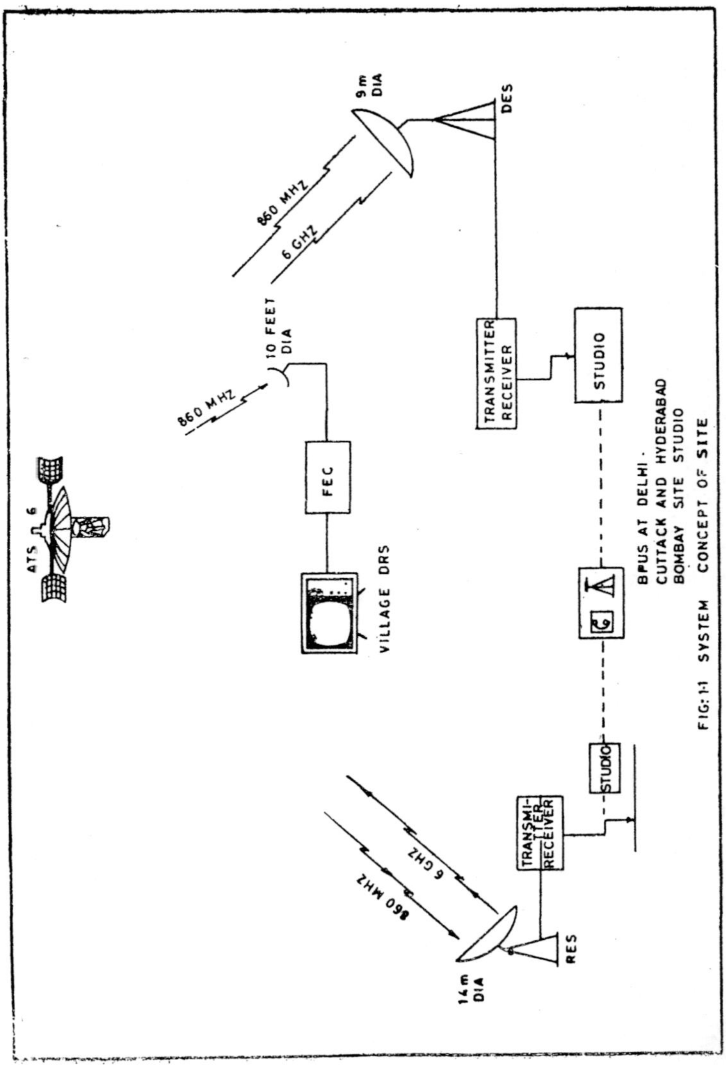

FIG. 1.1 : *System Concept of SITE*

Except for the half-hour common national programme, which was transmitted from the Delhi Earth Station, all other programmes were telecast from the Ahmedabad Earth Station. The national programme was during evening transmission only. Both morning and evening transmission schedules are given in Table 1.2.

TABLE 1.2 : **Transmission schedules in Bihar cluster**

Date	Timing
Morning Schedule	
1 August 1975 to 31 July 1976	11.7½—11.30 a.m.
Evening Schedule	
1 August 1975 to 31 October 1975	8.10—8.50 p.m.
1 November 1975 to 31 March 1976	6.00—7.00 p.m.
1 April 1976 to 31 July 1976	7.30—8.30 p.m.
National Programme	
1 August 1975 to 31 July 1976	7.00—7.30 p.m.

Maintenance of television sets

The television sets installed in 393 villages of Bihar cluster were maintained by the technical staff of the Space Applications Centre (ISRO) stationed at four maintenance sub-centres. In each village, a special television set known as Direct Reception System (DRS) was installed. DRS had three major components—a conventional television, a low noise pre-amplifier, and a three meter chicken-mesh parabolic antenna. All the television sets operated on 220 AC electric supply. On report of any fault in the Television set, the well-equiped staff visited the village and made necessary repairs.

Review of literature

The discussions on the role of communication in rural development have been reviewed in the following pages. Here, development means the betterment in the standard of living, increase in gross national product or in per capita income which are the basic indicators of economic development. This economic development is an extremely important factor because it enhances human development. Thus, it is a type of social change in which new ideas are introduced into the social system in order to produce higher per capita income.

Studies related to cultural communication in the context of television communication are limited in number.

Anthropology and communication

Outside India, Halls (1959) and Montague (1967) have discussed about the integral role of communication in a given culture. Kluckhohn (1961) described language as a tool of communication. Fischer (1973) highlighted the greater reliance of oral communication, especially in an illiterate society. Firth (1973) studied symbols, gestures and signs as types of communication for expressing ideas.

In India, Majumdar's study (1958) relates to *jati* and communication in a village of Lucknow district, Uttar Pradesh. Hitchcock (1963) studied process of socialization among the Rajputs of Khalapur, Uttar Pradesh which gives some ideas of culture communication. Gaikwad *et al.* (1973) analysed the process of inter-personal communication in a village of Raipur district, Madhya Pradesh.

While the above studies of Majumdar, Hitchcock and Gaikwad focus on inter-personal communication, Hein (1959) McCormack (1951), Damle (1959) and Gumperz (1964) have thrown light on the social value of the religious messages conveyed in different formats like *Katha, Kirtan, Ramleela* and other religious performances. Marriott (1959) noticed the changes in the traditional channels of communication as a result of introduction of mass media.

Communication and rural development

Talking on the development role of television, Lionberger (1958) finds it an effective tool for changing the cultivators' attitude to purchase of farm supplies recommended via the television. Dale (1963) holds the opinion that 10 minutes telecast on any agricultural practice is more effective than putting an extension man for a week. Alexander *et al.* (1963) found a significant increase in the knowledge of the cultivators in the field of cattle feeding practices when it was taught through the television. Referring to a study in Czechoslovakia, Hach (1967) reports television to be very useful for in-service training of staff members in an agricultural unit.

In India, the study on television started with the evaluation of Delhi Krishi Darshan programme. Mishra (1967), Sekhon (1968), Dey (1968), and the study conducted by National Council of Educational Research and Training (1968) found the viewers' characteristics as a responsible factor in the gain of farming knowledge and its proper utilization. On the other hand, Sinha (1974) identified the 'middle class' of cultivators as most receptive and said that this class is most ready for change. He also supported the two-step flow of information whereas Sankaria (1969) indicated a multi-step flow.

A number of evaluative studies have been conducted on SITE. Most of these studies, listed in the report of Gore (1979 : 37-40) are impact of programme specific studies. The study of Eapen (1979) analysed the role of television custodians, and user teachers' perception of school programme in Karnataka State. Singhi's study (nd), based on survey design, conducted at the end of SITE reveals that SITE reduced the knowledge gap between the rich and poor segments of population.

Chauhan and Sinha (1976 and 1977) credited televisions for increasing the level of adoption during SITE in Bihar villages. In another study Chauhan and Sinha (1979) tried to evaluate the impact of SITE television on the efficacy of the villagers towards norms. Sanga *et al.* (1979) point out that though the villagers are not aware of time/date schedule of the telecast of developmental programmes but are more aware about those developmental programmes which were telecast more frequently.

These studies in one way or other have indicated the positive role of television in rural development. It indicates that the major emphasis has been laid for measuring the impact on the television viewers. It seems, there is paucity of communication research related to process analysis. Recently, Sachchidananda and Jha (1980) and Agrawal (1981) have shown the potential advantages of process analysis in the understanding of the role of mass media in rural development. Keeping in view the above review, the present study attempts to understand the role and relevance of television in rural development. The general and specific objectives of the present study are defined below.

OBJECTIVES OF THE STUDY

This study was undertaken to provide a micro-level, in-depth, qualitative understanding of the process of socio-cultural changes triggered by the introduction of satellite television as a new medium of communication in a village of North Bihar. An eighteen-month fieldwork was conceived as a part of SITE Social Evaluation Study in which the author was responsible for carrying out the entire study. Part of the data for this work were collected in subsequent fieldwork, conducted in 1977 and 1980 summers. The general and specific objectives of the present study have been delineated. These are :

General objectives

To study the process of existing rural communication in a village of Bihar and its role in rural development;

To study the barriers of communication hindering rural development; and

To study the socio-cultural implications of a technological innovation like television.

Specific objectives

To study the utilization pattern of existing channels of communication for developmental and non-developmental activities in the village;

To study the rediffusion process of developmental messages in the village;

To study micro-level changes brought about by television in the village culture; and

To study the process of adoption of developmental messages.

2

METHODOLOGICAL STRATEGY

THERE is a great deal of argument regarding the methodology to be used in studying the role of any mass media. Sample survey to study the effects of media is a common practice in India and elsewhere. But, according to Rudolph and Rudolph (1960) survey has serious methodological limitations in eliciting correct responses. Blalock (1970) also holds the view that the survey method cannot be used to study actual behaviour, as it takes place. Harrison thinks that "... rigorous interview and questionnaire technique are entirely inappropriate in native villages ... village research is most productive if participant observation and informal survey methods are combined" (Harrison 1972 : 3). Forcese and Richer (1973 : 87) while comparing the usefulness of case study and survey method point out that the "case study offers in-depth data which often permit a researcher to follow up with more intelligent explanatory research". Black and Champion (1976) rate case studies to have greater utility in studying mobility pattern and interpersonal characteristics of small groups and communities.

Hence, it was thought that instead of measuring the impact of mass media in some pre-determined specific areas, an attempt should be made to understand the role of communication indepth while focusing on the life of the villagers of Ismailpur. In order to analyse the role of communication as a whole, it becomes imperative to follow a "research design" which would allow diachronic and continuous observations.

It is a safe assumption on the books and literature reviewed, that television messages are interpreted and understood within the cultural context. Therefore, it is essential to discover cultural judgements and various categories of the media message for cultural interpretation. Having this consideration in view, a methodological strategy, yielding the necessary data, became a challenge. It was decided to conduct a 'holistic study' in which the researcher would stay in one village for 18 months and study the communication process in a specific cultural context.

In the present study, the major emphasis has been to understand the process rather than to identify the structure. It is true that any process of change may differ according to society and the culture of the people, but "... change does not take place in a quixotic and unpredictable manner. Like all social phenomena, the events of culture modifications are patterned" (Foster 1962 : 28). According to him "... in all of us motivations to change are opposed by resistance of change" (Foster 1962 : 4). Thus, one of the major factor that determine any motivation towards change or resistance is psychological. Here attempts have been made to record the psychology of the villagers of Ismailpur and the corresponding responses of the viewers towards television communication.

Keeping these views in mind, the steps involved in conducting the study were :

Selection of the village ;
Methods and techniques to be followed in the data collection ;
Nature and quality of data to be collected ; and
Specific areas in which the focus should be directed towards obtaining answers to specific questions.

VILLAGE SELECTION

The revenue village was considered as a spatial unit for this study as most of the official records are only available for the "revenue village". A revenue village such as Pojha village of Goraul block may consist of only one main village of like Sondho of the same block the main village is surrounded by up to 20 hamlets. The entire settlement is named after the main village in the census or revenue records. This is a general problem throughout North Bihar and is not uncommon for the students of social sciences conducting researches in Indian villages.

The primary focus of observation, therefore, throughout the study is the revenue village whereas the fringe settlements which may not be part of the revenue village and from where people were expected to come to watch television are of secondary importance.

SITE was conducted in 393 villages of North Bihar, therefore, it was problem to select *one* village for the study. The question raised was how to select a village, representative of North Bihar. It was decided to base its holistic study in a district with the largest number of television sets. Accordingly, Muzaffarpur was chosen. At another level also, the important task was to select one representative village from Muzaffarpur district having 110 SITE villages. To narrow down the range of choice, the following criteria were taken into account in the selection of the village :

The population size of the village should be around 1,000 so that the researcher can have a face-to-face interaction with the total village population and conveniently observe them as closely as possible.

The village should be multi-*jati*, consisting of various *jatis* or religious groups to find out if a *jati* or religious group affiliation had any association with one's communication behaviour, and

The village should fall between a range of 29 to 30 kilometers away from an urban centre. This was to minimize any direct urban influence, thereby leading to a high communication exposure.

Keeping in view the population criteria, eleven villages were selected with the help of District Census Handbook—1961 from among 110 SITE villages in the district of Muzaffarpur. In the last week of January 1975, keeping in mind the above variables, nine villages of Kanti, Meenapur, Muraul, and Sakara development blocks of Muzaffarpur district were visited for the purpose of physical verification. The other two villages fell short of the distance criteria. The villages visited are given in Table 2.1.

Apart from other data collection, the visit was also meant to check whether accommodation would be available and whether the villagers would be willing to accept a researcher for a year and half.

After the actual field visits, which took about ten days, the researcher returned to Ahmedabad. A detailed discussion with colleagues was held on each village. The problem of village boundary and its implication for the study were also discussed and it was pointed out that in Rainy and Birpur villages the proposed television centres were in hamlets which were far from the main settlement.

TABLE 2.1 : **Villages visited for selection**

Name of the village	*Population 1961*	*Distance from Urban Centre*
Basatpur Jhitkahi	961	26 km
Birpur	1,353	22 km
Bisanpur Bakhari	914	29 km
Dardha	1,040	23 km
Harpur Krishna	866	24 km
Manika Harikisan	790	20 km
Mustafagunj	917	28 km
Parapur	841	25 km
Rainy	1,085	30 km

All the villages tentatively selected by the researcher in the first visit were found not suitable. The plea was that Mustafagunj and Parapur had scattered population leading to difficulty in the study and other villages were highly exposed to advance agricultural practices, being close to Agriculture College, Pusa. It would have led to a problem of studying the clear cut impact of agricultural programmes on the villagers, as shown on television. Now it was a problem for the researcher to reselect a village within a limited time. As there was no other alternative, it was decided to waive the distance criteria from the urban centre to the villages as 30 to 40 kilometers. Villages for selection could then be taken from Goraul block. On the basis of the data indicated in the census, it was finally decided that the village Ismailpur should be chosen for study without a prior visit.*

It had a population of 966 persons according to 1971 census, data provided by the Block Development Officer (BDO). It was hoped that by 1975 it would have increased to 1,000. This assumption was proved right when a door-to-door census was taken by the researcher. Ismailpur fulfilled all the criteria suggested earlier, except the original distance criteria. The village is at a distance of 37 kilometers south of Muzaffarpur. It is 9 kilometers away from block office and has seven Hindu *jatis* and Muslim population (*see* Chapter 3).

* The details given in the SITE village-selection-survey-schedule and researcher's own experience as a team member of SITE village-selection-team helped the decision-making.

Training

Before coming to field, the researcher had to attend a pre-data collection training to understand communication process in village India, the theoretical and methodological basis of the study and the understanding of the role of television in a community-viewing situation. During the training, each concept used was operationally defined (described later). Areas and priorities were also defined for the purpose of data collection in the various phases of the study. Thereafter the researcher went to Delhi for one week training in National Council of Educational Research and Training (NCERT) to learn about the method of observing child psychology and child behaviour in the school. By this time, it was end of February, 1975 and the researcher entered the village of Ismailpur on March 1975 to start the fieldwork.

The total work was divided into three phases of data collection : pre-SITE, during-SITE, and post-SITE.

Impression management

After meeting the Block Development Officer at Goraul the researcher came down to the village with a man of neighbouring village. From village-selection-survey-schedule it was known that the village has one Panchayat (village council) building and one community hall, so he approached to the Mukhia (village council chief) for accommodation in the community hall. Initially, for two days he stayed in Mukhias' out-house and then shifted to the community hall which was utilized for keeping fertilizers and fodder.

While cleaning and organizing the room, a few youths came forward to help the researcher and became friendly. With their help, the researcher acquainted himself with the streets and introduced himself to the villagers. He introduced himself as a research scholar from the Television Department but tried his best to make it very clear that even though he had some connection with the television, he was not at all concerned with the operation and maintenance of the television. Rather he has come to study the village culture and the impact of television on it. As he knew the language of this region and belonged to the numerically dominant *jati*-Awadhiya, he was gladly welcomed by the villagers. The Awadhiya accepted the researcher as a member of their group on *jati*-basis. But, when he started going and meeting the lower *jatis* and Harijan households, the old men of the Awadhiya *jati* tried to impress upon him not to do so. This act of the researcher surprised the lower *jati* and Harijan villagers who praised him for his cordial and familial behaviour. But at the same time, they also criticised the Awadhiyas for their rude treatment to them. Some young boys of Awadhiya *jati* also followed the researcher's way and started sitting with the lower *jati* people.

In the beginning, the villagers and the block officials did not believe that an educated and city man would stay in this village for a year and half. But when the researcher started cooking and managing his establishment, they formed a different opinion about him. Initially the Mukhia (village council chief) tried to patronise the researcher by showing off his socio-economic and political influences in and outside the village. He wanted him to teach his sons and offered free accommodation and food. The community hall was meant for VLW so some of the villagers took him as VLW. In the past, one compounder stayed in this building, hence the poor women of labour households came to the researcher with their difficulties and ailments and asked for medicine.

The researcher's door-to-door census work gave him status of other government servants who sometimes come for population and livestock census. His presence around television, when it was on, associated his identity with television department of Government of India and writing of daily diary till late night put many of them into doubt. Whenever, the block officials or SITE staff from maintenance sub-centre would come to this side, they came to see the welfare of the researcher which strengthened the doubt of his being a very high officer in government cadre.

In took almost three to four months when villagers were convinced about his harmlessness and accepted him as a member of the village. Afterwards he was invited on all occasions and he shared the joy and sorrow of the village. He worked as a negotiator for marriages, he was invited to settle many quarrels in the village, he was made director of the drama staged by the village youth, and also he was asked for any information on any sphere of life.

In the first week of March 1975, the deserted community hall was made the residence of the researcher. This house was very near to the television centre. It was the central point from Dhuntoli and Southern ward but isolated in the sense that there was no other house around 50 meters radius. Being at the bank of the canal, it was a place where villagers used to sit to watch fishes in the morning and the evening.

The room had door towards north and windows towards north, south and east. The villagers' activities in these directions were easily to be observed while sitting in the room.

Researcher's morning started with a preliminary round in the streets ; observing general activities and asking welfare of the villagers. After breakfast, he went to meet informants in their homes, fields, or gardens. In the noon when he remained at home preparing meal, taking lunch, or relaxing, villagers would come to him to take water from him or to chat with him. These villagers were mostly the youth or the cultivators and labourers who were working in the nearby field and wanted to relax and chew tobacco. Afternoon was devoted in collecting specific data, particularly from cultivators and women informants. Evening was spent in preparing night meal, entertaining people and attending different gossip groups. During the SITE programme it changed into watching television and observing viewers' activities and then collecting feed back on programme or some information concerning the telecast. The writing of notes and diary could be done only when it was late night and the visitors left him alone. But this routine got disturbed many times due to reasons such as appointment with some informant, some special events in the village, lunch/dinner with some villager, and prolonged sitting in the gossip groups.

There ware also some seasonal variations. During summer, it was exempted to minimize the movements in scorching heat while during winter early movements and late night talks were accommodated during the day time.

Pre-SITE data collection

The first task after getting accommodation and having a formal introduction to the villagers was to conduct a door-to-door census and to prepare a village map. It took nearly one and half months to complete the census work with generalogies and mapping of the village. The village map shows the location of all the houses, important places, lanes, fields, and village electrification (*see* village map on page 27). During this time, the researcher established closer rapport with the villagers and could collect data on village life in general. From May 1975, the specific data on social structure, channels of communication, political organisation and economic structure was collected through participant and non-participant observations, discussions, and interviews. Emphasis was given to record the centres and sources of different types of information. This included investigating various methods that were used for the purpose of transmitting messages through travelling musicians, vendors, village quacks, collective listening of religious and mythological hymns, incoming and outgoing postal mails, and a host of inter-personal channels of communications that are used in the village for the purpose of passing information among the relatives, friends, *jati*-members, and others.

DURING-SITE DATA COLLECTION

With the commencement of SITE in August 1975 the aim was to focus on the television and its related activities *vis-a-vis* the villagers. As many programmes as possible, were viewed during the SITE period to observe the audience behaviour. The researcher's activities centered around morning and evening television viewing, observation of post-telecast discussions and participation of the day-to-day life of the village. He tried to trace out the message diffusion process.

A daily observation sheet was designed to plot the sitting pattern and note down the viewing behaviour of the villagers by sex, *jati*, and age. It helped in knowing the changes in viewing and sitting pattern, audience size and its composition. During the viewing periods, the researcher tried to collect data on this sheet noting down the names of the programmes and viewer response towards it. A daily attendance register was also maintained and on the basis of these the 'core audience' and 'target audience' were identified. Some village youth helped in this venture.

The family planning data were also collected to know the villagers' attitude towards family size and social value of son and daughter.

Within a single village, those who did not view television (non-viewer) were to be compared with those who did television (viewer) for the purpose of assessing the effects and also for comparing the process of change among the viewers and non-viewers.

A Multi-Media Package Training Programme for Science Teachers in the month of October 1975 was organized. The television, was viewed and the reaction of the teachers were taken into account to evaluate the training programme. The broad questions investigated were—the television utilization pattern during the training, the general observation about the training organization at the village level, and the trainees' opinion on the utility and usefulness of the training programme. Operation, coordination, and management aspects of the training were also studied in detail.

POST-SITE DATA COLLECTION

The researcher continued to live in the village for another two months after the SITE programme was over and continued observing the villagers' reactions to the withdrawal of television. Observations were focused to note if there were any changes in the village after the television ceased functioning from 1 August, 1976. Emphasis was given to the study of the continuity of impact brought out by television and also how the television viewers re-adjusted their evening time which they used to spend viewing television.

Throughout the data collection, *emic* approach* had been followed in order to avoid any data distortion. Case studies of observed changes among viewers and non-viewers were also recorded.

Photographs were taken to record the different aspects of village life and audio cassettes were used for recording songs, music, and dialogues. Secondary data were collected from various offices concerned with development at panchayat, block as well as at the district level. Data from the school and the post office were collected through the official register and researcher himself checked the authenticity of the figures entered in the registers.

Some of the preliminary findings were presented in two SITE Social Evaluation workshops held at Ahmedabad in the middle of 1975 and 1976. The opinions and suggestions of the participants : eminent anthropologists, sociologists, communication experts were taken into account while collecting further data.

POST-SITEVISITS

Two short spells of fieldwork were conducted after the initial intensive fieldwork of 19 months. This fieldwork was undertaken in June-July 1977 and May-June 1980. Broadly, the researcher was interested in collecting supplementary data to study the process of

* According to Harris, "emic statements refer to logico-empirical systems whose phenomenal distinction or things are built up out of contrasts and discriminations significant, meaningful, real, accurate, or in some other fashion recorded as appropriate by the actors themselves" (Harris 1968 : 571).

adoption of innovation as a result of television viewing. As the May-June 1980 fieldwork coincided with the Bihar Assembly election, the researcher was in a position to observe the role of interpersonal communication in decision-making. The specific data on the Multi-Purpose Cooperative Society (*see* Chapter 4) and Yuva Dal (*see* Chapter 10) were collected.

In the revisits, the origional census data was used for the purpose of analysis. Also the researcher stayed in the villages as a guest instead of resident scholar, as was done during the first visit. A majority of the villagers took the researcher's visit as a summer vacation visit. The rapport built earlier was rejuvenated on subsequent visits.

It can be said that this study is the outcome of 22 months fieldwork, in which the researcher was present in the villages for 548 days, but 116 days he was out of village for personal as well as other reasons like attending the seminars, collecting secondary data, and attending cluster head office.

In this chapter, the methodological strategy of data collection for this thesis has been described. Major emphasis was laid or participant observation and case study approach, keeping in view the objectives of the study for the understanding of the process of communication. In the next two chapters, the profile of the village will be presented.

OPERATIONAL DEFINITIONS

Prior to the fieldwork, and during the fieldwork, the most difficult part was, and continues to be, the definition of the various emic categories used for the purpose of description and analysis. To have a conceptual clarity, operational definitions of each of the concepts have been presented and are followed thoughout this work.

Jati : The term *jati* is used to denote an endogamous, intermarrying, extended and regional group. A similar concept also exists among non-Hindus. Therefore, the term '*Jati*-like' will be used to refer to the similar Muslim group.

Household

In emic terms the 'family' is referred to as *ghar* in Hindi. In this report the term 'household' has been used to denote *ghar*, operationally defined as those persons living and eating together who may or may not be relatives.

With experts

Discussion

With SITE team

With development agent

Interview

With labourer

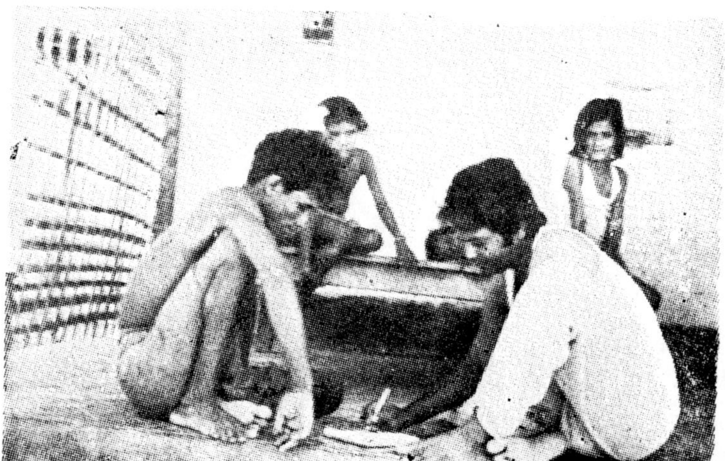

Process of communication

The emphasis, here is on the undertaking of the process of communication. According to Wallace (1970 : 100) :

> Processes have in common the property that time, and often physical space too, is a dimension of the structure, and that the structure is divided into a sequence of steps or stages corresponding to the successive values on the time/space dimension. Each stage then can be considered as a single value on a dimension that corresponds precisely in number of values to the time/space dimension ; but each of these values on the stage dimension can be decomposed into a complex structure whose matrix may be (but is not necessarily) unique to that stage.

In the communication context, the programmes shown on television were seen by a limited range of viewers who in turn discussed what they had seen with other non-viewers. The non-viewers, in turn, discussed with other non-viewers. In this case, a three-steps flow of communication is indicated, with each stage defined by persons who act as mediators between the information and the receivers of the information. Certain amount of information gets modified, changed or distorted before reaching the next person. It seems that these processual structures contain three kinds of dimensions – time/space a 'core matrix'—information that is shared by all stages, though, it may get transformed while moving from one stage to another stage. The third dimension is the 'peripheral metrix'—television viewer/non-viewer. 'The peripheral matrices are relevant only in some of the stage.'

Wallace (1970 : 101) feels that "some simple structure can have only the first two stages". In the present discussion, all the three dimensions will be considered and analysed while discussing the process of communication. In most cases, it will be implicit, but from time to time, it will be made explicit.

School children

The term 'school children' refers to those who attend primary school. In this case they are between 5-13 years of age studying up to third grade.

Adult

The term 'adult', male and female, is operationally defined as all those who are of 14 years of age at the time of census taking in the village.

Children

From time to time, data are categorised into two major age groups—children and adults. When the term children alone is used, it refers to all those are 14 years of age and below.

Viewers

The term 'viewers' or 'frequent viewers' has been operationally defined as those who view television more than four times a month.

Core viewers

The term 'core viewer' is used for those adults who viewed programmes more than two-thirds of the time when the television was operational in a month.

3

ISMAILPUR : THE VILLAGE

IN THE previous chapter, the method and techniques that were followed in this study have been described. In this chapter, the profile of Ismailpur has been depicted.

THE REGION

The district of Muzaffarpur (old), forming a part of North Bihar plains, is centrally located in the Tirhut division. It comprises an extensive plain created over the years by the alluvium deposits of the Ganga, the Gandak, and other river systems which flow through this region. North Bihar plain has large traits of low lying lands which are very fertile and productive for crops. The soil of this region is highly calcarious. Among the other different kinds of soil found here are sandy, loamy, light clayey, and *usar*. Paddy is grown mostly on clayey land whereas loam is particularly suited for *rabi* crops.

The district is rich in vegetation and its green fields are dotted with grooves of mango, bamboo, and other trees. The land being fertile, no area has been left for wild growth now. On the ridges of the ditches *muni* (*saccharum munja*) reed plantations grow. And in low-lying lands, partially submerged in water from August to March, aquatic plants spring up.

The region has a dry and healthy climate with three seasons—winter, summer and monsoon. Winter begins in early November and last till March. January is the coldest month of the season. The temperature begins to rise from March and the maximum is attained in May. The heat is intense until the rains set in around the middle of June or early July. The normal rainfall of the district is 1180 mm. per year.

LOCATION

In this geographical region, Ismailpur is one of the many villages located at 25.9° north latitude and 85.4° east longitude and lies in Goraul block of the newly-created Vaishali district of old Muzaffarpur district. It is the headquarters of Ismailpur *panchayat* (village council) and falls under Goraul Police Station range and Sondho postal jurisdiction.

Ismailpur is situated 37 kilometers south of Muzaffarpur town. Up to Goraul, it is connected both by railway and state highway. The village is nine kilometers south-east of Goraul, out of which four kilometers is metalled road which connects Baghi. From Sondho (a mid-point on the metal road) one factory approach road starts and five kilometer later this fair weather jeepable road reaches Ismailpur. This village can also be approached by Muzaffarpur-Mahua-Hajipur road and it is at a distance of four kilometers from Dullahpur bus stop. Owing to the poor road facilities, the means of transportation are bicycle, *tumtum* (horse cart), and bullock cart.

When one comes to the fair weather *kutcha* road, from Goraul side, the first revenue village Sondho is seen which is spread for about two and half km. in length. This village is fairly large in size and a tri-weekly market is held in this village. Next to Sondho comes Paigamberpur followed by Ismailpur. In south of Ismailpur are Majhia, Khokhara, Premraj, and Chakfatteh villages, all within a kilometer distance. All these villages form a continuous habitation and are connected to each other. A cart track demarcates the boundaries of Ismailpur and Fattehpur villages on north-eastern side. It is difficult to separate southern boundary of Ismailpur from Majhia village as the cattle houses of both the villages are intermingled. The factory approach road passes through Ismailpur from north to south.

LANGUAGE

Ismailpur is a village in the Hindi-speaking area, but the dialect is Bajjika which is a mixture of Magahi, Maithili and Bhojpuri dialects of Hindi language. Most of the villagers, except the literates, speak only Bajjika and no other dialect. Villagers, specially women, find it difficult to understand Hindi. Semi-literates (up to primary standard) also have difficulty in understanding Hindi). The literates speak and understand Hindi well but prefer Bajjika. There is nobody in the village who can speak any language other than Hindi.

SETTLEMENT PATTERN

The land of Ismailpur is divided into *Chaur* (low land), *Bheeth* (high elevation land), and *Nasi* (land with a little slope). Chaur is water-logged from August to March and during the rainy season it looks link a large pond. *Bheeth* is used for habitation and tobacco cultivation. *Nasi* is used as cultivable land for *rabi* and *kharif* crops but tobacco is not cultivated on it (*see* figure 3.1).

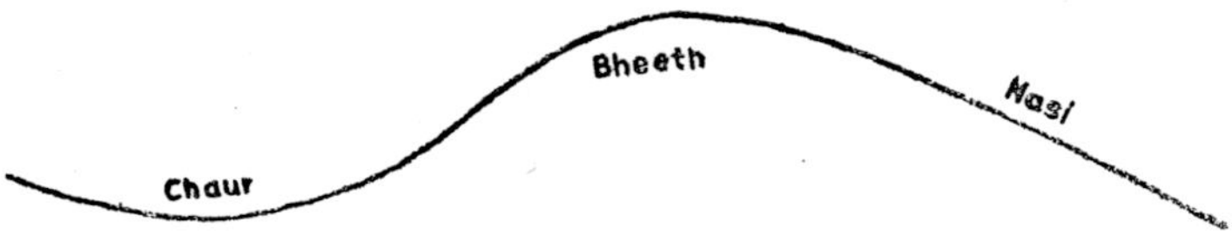

FIG. 3.1 : *Land Profile of Ismailpur*

All the houses are constructed on the *Bheeth* land on either side of the road. This is a general settlement pattern of this area. However, due to an increase in population, few houses have also been built on *Nasi* land in the recent past (*see* Village Map page 27).

Out of eight wards, six wards are located on the east side of the road whereas two wards are located to the west side. However, there are no inter-connecting streets between the wards. Each ward is inhabited by a *jati* and is referred by its *jati's* name or geographical location. As the Awadhiya *jati* is numerically most dominant, they occupy four wards. The *Purbari tola* (Eastern Ward), being the recent one, is the only ward where three *jatis* are living together (*see* Table 3.1).

TABLE 3.1 : **Distribution of households and population according to ward**

Name of Wards	*No. of Households*	*Population*
Uttarbaritola (Northern Ward)	20	147
Awadhiyan	40	256
Hazamtoli (Hazam Ward)	37	197
Pachhiyari tola (Western Ward)	8	48
Purbari tola (Eastern Ward)	9	45
Dhuntoli (Dhunia Ward)	22	86
Dakhinwari tola (Southern Ward)	28	198
Binkharia	8	39
Total	172	1,016

TYPES OF HOUSES

House types, to a large extent, indicate the relative socio-economic status of its occupants ; the lowest form of construction being huts and the highest being *pucca* houses. Ismailpur has four types of house construction : (1) Hut—thatched roof and walls (2) *Kutcha* house—mud walls with tiled roof (3) Semi-*pucca* house—brick walls with tiled roof, and (4) *Pucca* house—brick wall and *pucca* (concrete) roof. Table 3.2 shows that only 5.2 per cent are *pucca* houses whereas 22.7 per cent are huts. The most predominant house types found in the village is *kutcha* houses (43%).

TABLE 3.2 : **Percentage distribution according to types of houses in Ismailpur**

House Type		*No. of Households*	*Percentage*
Hut		39	22.7
Kutcha house		74	43.0
Semi-*pucca* house		50	29.1
Pucca house		9	5.2
	Total	172	100.0

The houses lack ventilation and are shared by both men and their cattle. The cattle are generally kept near the house during summer and winter whereas they are accommodated inside the houses during the rainy season. Food grains, fodder and agricultural implements are also kept in the same dwelling. In the absence of a drainage system, every household throws its waste at the rear side of the house.

VILLAGE POPULATION

There are 1,016 persons (509 males and 507 females) in the village according to the census taken in April 1975. The total number of the households divided into eight different wards is 172. The village has both Hindu and Muslim population. The Hindu belong to seven *jatis* forming 79.1 per cent of the total population whereas the Dhunia (Muslim) constitute remaining 20.9 per cent of the population (*see* Table 3.3).

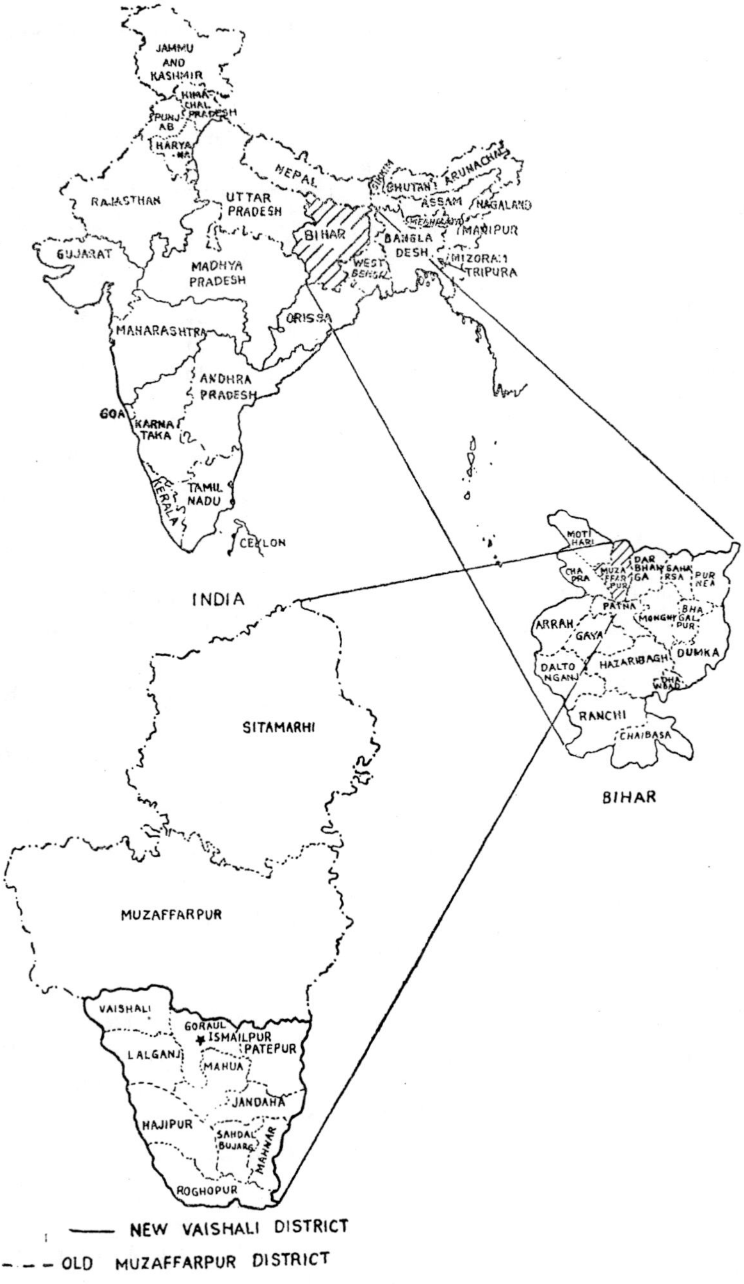

FIG 3.2 : *Location of Ismailpur in national perspective*

TABLE 3.3 : **Distribution of jati and jati-like groups according to sex and religion**

Jati/Jati-like	*No. of Households*	*Male*	*Female*	*Total*
Hindu				
Awadhiya	82	307	254	561
Magahiya Teli	12	36	43	79
Madesia Kanoo	10	38	29	67
Awadhia Hazam	13	24	36	60
Kharmat Nonia	11	23	29	52
Magahiya Dusadh	5	13	10	23
Rahmani Kahar	3	5	10	15
Muslim				
Khaje Mansoor Dhunia	36	63	96	159
Total	172	509	507	1,016

Awadhiya *jati* is numerically the most dominant *jati* having little over 55 per cent of the total village population. If one ranks these *jatis* according to relative social hierarchy, they can be ranked as : (i) Awadhiya (ii) Teli (iii) Kanoo (iv) Hazam (v) Nonia (vi) Kahar, and (vii) Dusadh (scheduled caste.)

Broadly, these *jatis* can be categorised into four hierarchical groups. They are :

(1) High *Jati*—Awadhiya
(2) Intermediate—*Jati*—Teli and Kanoo
(3) Low *Jati*—Hazam, Nonia, Dhunia*, and Kahar
(4) Scheduled Caste—Dusadh

Table 3.4 shows the distribution of population according to age groups. More than 40 per cent of the village population is below 15 years of age whereas little less than 10 per cent is above 55 years. The remaining population falls between 15 to 54 years of age which is, according to the villagers, the age when one can lookafter household work.

* The *jati*-like group of Muslim e.g. Dhunia has been placed among low *jati* as they are ranked by the villagers in this category.

The Village Ismailpur

The Transport

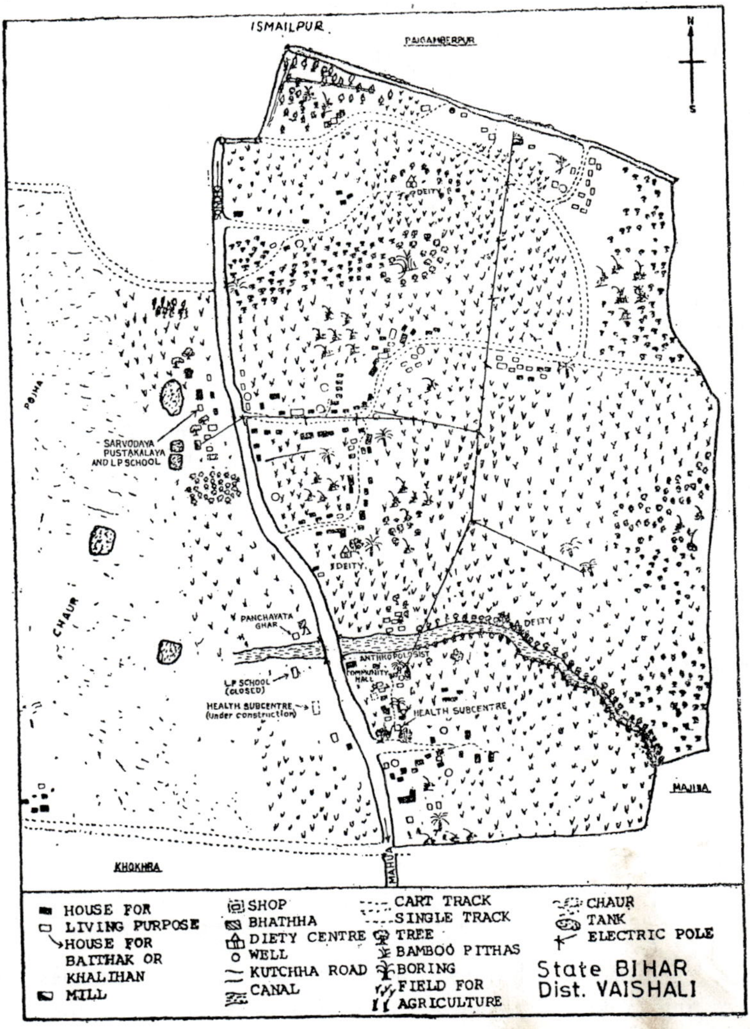

FIG. 3.3 : *Ismailpur village*

TABLE 3.4 : **Percentage distribution of population according to age groups**

Age Group	*No. of Persons*	*Percentage*	
0—4 years	131	12.9	
5—14 years	316	31.1	44.0
15—24 years	150	14.8	
25—34 years	140	13.8	46.3
35—44 years	109	10.7	
45—54 years	71	7.0	
55 years and above	99	9.7	9.7
Total	1,016	100.0	100.0

Table 3.5 shows percentage distribution of households according to household size and religion. The model distribution fall between two to five members per household (51.7%) followed by 30.8 per cent households having six to nine members. On both extremes, a little over four per cent households are 'unimember' of '14 and more members household'. In general, large proportion of households in Ismailpur are those below five members.

TABLE 3.5 : **Percentage distribution according to household size and religion**

Household Size	*Religion*		*Total*
	Hindu	*Muslim*	
1	2.9	11.1	4.7
2—5	47.9	69.3	51.7
6—9	35.5	14.0	30.8
10—13	9.5	5.6	8.7
14+	5.1	0.0	4.1
Total	79.1	20.9	100.0

Table 3.6 shows distribution of household size by *jati* categories. It is interesting to note that there seems to be an association between *jati* hierarchy and household size. High *jati* has the highest per cent of household having more than five members (57.4%). Opposite to this low *jatis* have more than 65 per cent of households having two to five members.

TABLE 3.6 : **Percentage distribution of household size by jati categories**

Household Size	*Jati Categories*				
	High jati	*Inter-mediate jati*	*Low jati*	*Scheduled Caste*	*Total*
1	2.4	0.0	7.9	20.0	4.7
2—5	40.2	58.2	66.8	60.0	51.7
6—9	41.6	27.2	20.5	0.0	30.8
10—13	8.5	10.1	4.8	20.0	8.7
14+	7.3	4.5	0.0	0.0	4.1
Total	47.7	12.8	36.6	2.9	100.0

ECONOMY

The major source of income of Ismailpur is based on agriculture. As described later in this chapter, it is a non-*jati* associated economic activity.

Table 3.7 shows that more than 50 per cent of the village population depends upon agriculture, which is the major source of livelihood. Not only agriculturists but the labourers are also dependent on agriculture. They put their maximum effort in it and grow as much as they can. The fields of Ismailpur are not seen to be barren during the agricultural period. The improved agriculture and pressing need for more food has changed the growing pattern.

TABLE 3.7 : **Percentage distribution of households according to jati categories and primary occupation**

Occupation	*High Jati*	*Inter-mediate Jati*	*Low Jati*	*Schedule Caste*	*Total*
Cultivation	90.2	45.4	3.2	0.0	50.0
Labour	1.2	27.3	55.5	100.0	27.4
Business	1.2	27.3	11.1	0.0	8.1
Professional Employment	6.2	0.0	14.3	0.0	8.1
Jati-Related occupation	0.0	0.0	15.9	0.0	5.8
No Work	1.2	0.0	0.0	0.0	0.6
Total	47.7	12.8	36.6	2.9	100.0

Table 3.8 gives an idea of cropping pattern of Ismailpur. Tobacco is the main cash crop. Previously, when Goraul sugar mill was running, sugarcane was grown in large quantity and it was considered as the second important cash crop. But, after the closure of the sugar mill in 1966, cultivators have reduced growing sugarcane. Other crops grown in the village are oilseed and pulses.

TABLE 3.8 : **Yearly crop pattern in Ismailpur**

Name of the Crop	*No. of Crops*	*Time of the Crops*
Maize	Three Crops	(i) October-March (ii) February-August (iii) July-October
Paddy	Two Crops	(i) August-December (ii) April-July
Wheat	One Crop	(i) November-March
Tobacco	One Crop	(i) October-March
Sugarcane	One Crop	(i) November-November

The agricultural land is owned by Awadhiya, Teli, Kanoo and Hazam *jatis*. The land-holding of these cultivators differs from one acre to 20 acres. Only 1.7 per cent of the total households own land more than 10 acres where 28.5 per cent are landless and 50 per cent cultivators own from half an acre to five acres of land (*see* Table 3.9).

TABLE 3.9 : **Percentage distribution of household land holding by Jati categories**

Land-holding	*High jati*	*Inter-mediate jati*	*Low Jati*	*Scheduled Caste*	*Total*
Landless	0.0	4.5	74.6	20.0	28.5
Marginal (Less than one acre)	8.5	45.5	22.2	80.0	20.3
Small (2-3 acres)	56.1	18.2	1.6	0.0	29.7
Medium-small (4-5 acres)	13.4	27.3	0.0	0.0	9.9
Medium (6-10 acres)	18.3	4.5	1.6	0.0	9.9
Large (10-20 acres)	3.7	0.0	0.0	0.0	1.7
Very large (21 +)	0.0	0.0	0.0	0.0	0.0
Total	47.7	12.8	36.6	2.9	100.0

There are three types of cultivators in Ismailpur :

Owner

Owners are those who do not put their own labour but get the work done under their supervision. Only 1.7 per cent households of Awadhiya *jati* come under this category. They employ temporary as well as permanent labourers. The temporary or daily wage labourers get fixed wages and the permanent servants, who are locally known as *jan*, get a monthly salary apart from two meals, clothes, and a little piece of cultivable land as long he serves the master. In one household, the supervision work is also done by a permanent servant.

Owner-Cultivator

In Ismailpur, 49.5 per cent of the total households, fall under the category of owner-cultivator. They work themselves in the field and whenever they need additional help they employ daily wage labourers. This happens mainly during transplantation, weeding, and harvesting periods.

Cultivator-Labourer

In this category are such cultivators who do not have sufficient land to support the family. Nearly 20 per cent come in this category who own less than one acre of land. They are engaged in some sort of part-time jobs like bullock cart driving, selling grains in tri-weekly market, labour work in other's field, and any other miscellaneous work. Only three households practice share cropping.

Five Teli households have their own *kolhus* (oil extracting machine) as a source of income. However, they are mainly cultivators and do tobacco business. The trading business is the main source of income for 8 per cent of the households, whereas 8.8 per cent households of barber persue traditional occupation of hair cutting and hair dressing in Muzaffarpur, Darjeeling, and other cities and send money from there to the members of their households. Eight Nonia households have their side business of *khar* (refined alkaline soil) preparation which they prepare out of calcareous soil during the month of March and April.

Selling vegetables and other grains in the village market in a partial support to the economy and elderly women from all *jatis* go with their produce sit in the market, sell the same and come back with the money or may purchase some requirements.

Service of pumping set on hire also support atleast five households of Awadhiya and Teli *jatis*. The daily wage for male is rupees three and for female rupees two alongwith a meal at noon. But generally, cultivators engage women for half day and pay rupee one only. The wage increases according to nature of work like transplanting rupees five a day. Harvesting is done by paying 1/16th amount of the harvested crop to the labourer.

POLITICAL ORGANISATION

After the abolition of the *jamindari* system, the *Panchayat Raj* was introduced. In Panchayat Raj system, the district Vaishali has eleven blocks. Each block sends an elected panchayat representative to form a district board headed by a Chairman. The Goraul Block has altogether 26 panchayats and Ismailpur is one of them which includes six other villages. The administration of this panchayat shifted from the hand of an ex-Muslim landlord to an elected panchayat representative. However, the same Muslim ex-landlord was elected Mukhia (panchayat chief) in 1959. In subsequent elections, an Awadhiya won the elections of 1962 and 1967. So, since 1962, this Awadhiya continues to be Mukhia whereas ex-Muslim landlord continues to be *Sarpanch* (Head Jury of the village council). Mukhia belongs to Ismailpur village and Sarpanch is from Majhia village. Mukhia is representing the block in the district board since March 1976.

In the village, there are two distinct 'factional groups' ; one is pro-Mukhia and the other is anti-Mukhia. Anti-Mukhia group is headed by a man, locally known as Naradji, in alliance with Teli, Awadhiya and Nonia *jatis*. Rest of *jatis* are not involved in any political activity. Within the village, the informal leader Naradji has a strong hold, and in almost all the panchayats of any *jati*, he will be one of the judges.

Prior to 1970, these two leaders were close friends. It is believed that they shared bounties of several shady deals. But in one of such deals, they quarrelled on distribution. Since then, they have been apart.

The various *jatis* living in Ismailpur do not have their separate *jati* panchayats. In local disputes, special panchayats are constituted in which Naradji is a permanent fixture. It is because he is available in the village and the mukhia, being a busy man stays very little in the village and he is also unable to respond to the needs of the village. Very few cases go to court for settlement. Few Awadhiya *jati* men are sympathisers of ruling party. It is to counter act to the Mukhia as he is associated with opposition party.

It seems there is very little influence of formal political system on the lives of the villagers.

RELIGION AND RELIGIOUS LIFE

Two religious groups namely, Hindu and Muslim are living in the village. Among the Hindus, Lord Rama, Krishna, and Shiva are worshipped and many festivals are celebrated. Dhunias pray to Allah and read the Quran. They observe *Id-ul-fitr*, *Bakr-id*, *Muharram*, and *Ramzan* festivals.

The village does not have any temple. Both the Hindus and Muslims worship Goddess Jagadamba and God Malang Baba for fulfilment of their desires. On any auspicious occasion, like the first hair-shaving ceremony, marriage, or birth, they worship these deities apart from their household deities. It had been observed that the festivals like *Astajam* and *Muhharram* were equally enjoyed by both the Hindu and the Muslim people. The Hindus also observe festivals like Holi, Teej, Chakchanda, Nag Panchami, Chhatha, and Saraswati Puja. Holi is the most enjoyable festival of the Hindus.

It was observed that most of the festivals are celebrated by Awadhiya, Teli and Hazam *jatis*. Males of the Awadhiya, Teli, and Hazam *jatis* have completed *Kanwar Yatra* (sacred water walk) in Muzaffarpur, whereas two cultivators have travelled up to Baidyanathdham and Tarkeshwarnath. The concept of rebirth and *moksha* (salvation) is widely prevalent in Ismailpur.

For the welfare of the cattle, all the *jatis* and even the Dhunias worship Bhuiyan Baba once in a year on the occasion of the first day of *Kartika* (October-November). On that occasion, some of them offer the entire morning milk to God Langa-Subhai at Sonepur.

We find Ismailpur as a representative village of old Muzaffarpur, North Bihar. The land profile is typical of this region where houses and streets are built on the elevated land. It gives a picture of rural Bihar where most of the people live in *kutcha* houses and majority of labourers spend their lives in huts. The average household size is between two to five members. The heterogeneous composition of the village allows all high, intermediate, and low *jatis*. Both the Hindu and Muslim population live together and participate in social as well as religious activities.

The villagers speak only Bajjika dialect of the Hindi language. The literacy rate is low and the illiterates find it difficult to speak and understand Hindi.

The village population of 172 households mainly depends upon agriculture and allied activities engaging over 25 per cent labour households. Of course, some households are doing business, *jati*-related occupation, and professional employment to support the household economy. The village economy rotates around agriculture, particularly the cash crop, tobacco. The land-holding size is small and only 1.7 per cent of the total households own land more than 10 acres whereas 28.5 per cent are landless. The cultivators are of different categories—owner, own-cultivator, and cultivator-labourer.

Political consciousness have not effected the general life of the village, rather these are confined to the Mukhia and a few other well to do Awadhiya households. A variety of fairs and festivals are celebrated by both the Hindu and the Muslim.

4

HEALTH AND EDUCATION

IN THE previous chapter, we have discussed the village profile with special focus on its agro-based economy. The present chapter will describe the aspects related to health, education and general infrastructure in the village.

FOOD AND FOOD HABITS

Rice, maize and wheat are commonly used as staple food along with locally grown pulses and green vegetables. Small quantity of fish available from ponds and canals, and even snails are also consumed by the poor.

Rice is boiled in water and taken along with pulses, vegetables, and occasionally only with salt and oil. Maize has its three general types of preparation—(a) ground maize is used for making baked bread which villagers eat with vegetable and sometimes with salt only ; (b) roughly ground maize is boiled along with water and the paste, locally known as *ghattha,* is taken with a little quantity of salt and onion ; and (c) the roasted maize is ground and the powder is mixed with water and used. It is said that some 10 to 15 years ago, consuming rice and wheat was a status symbol. But now the prices of all grains and commodities have gone up, so everyone purchases rice or wheat, as maize is not cheap any more. However, the consumption of maize is more compared to other grains because it is produced locally.

Only a few rich families buy vegetables from the market, otherwise they eat whatever they produce by themselves. In most of the households, vegetables are grown in a *bari* (kitchen garden). Banana is used as a vegetable which is generally available throughout the year.

Milk and curd are available to some of the cultivator households. But for the poor villagers, it is a source of earning money, so they sell it either to the rich villagers or to the tea-stalls in the village and outside.

During August to January most of the villagers catch small fish from the canal and utilize these daily. They either roast the fish or prepare fish curry. Eggs are not easily available in this area, but are preferred by most of the young Awadhiyas whereas the old Awadhiyas consider it as a food of the Muslims. Thus, we can see that a majority of the villagers, except some old Awadhiyas are non-vegetarians.

On important occasions or when some guests are invited, Awadhiya women prepare *puree* (fried flat bread) and *kheer* (porridge).

Most of the men in the village drink toddy. Some villagers either remove fresh toddy from the palm tree and drink it there itself or consume the toddy in their houses. Many villagers have the habit of chewing raw tobacco and smoke *bidis*. The youth have taken to smoking cigarettes of late.

In labour households, meals are taken twice in a day ; once at noon and another after evening work. The left overs of the previous night is given to the children in the morning. In other households, the children take 'breakfast' in the morning and meals at noon and evening. Adults generally take meals in the morning, at noon and evening. During summer, they take fried maize or rice along with onion and salt in the evening, if the night meal is served late.

HEALTH

The health of the villagers in general is good and they correlate it with the purity of air and good food. If anybody is weak or not keeping good health, he is subject to the criticism that he does not take a full diet or that he is a miser. But if one has some disease in spite of all care and medical facilities available to him, people correlate it with *karma* which has appeared in the form of punishment through disease. The canal and village pond are being used for bathing by most of the villagers. At the same time these places are also used for bathing cattle, washing utensils as well as clothes. Soap is being used by some of the villagers. Ladies use soap more than the males whereas washing soaps are used more than toilet soaps. For cleaning of clothes, washing soda is also in use and the poor villagers sometimes use alkaline soil. Many persons have been found taking their bath after 7 to 10 days,

Disease and folk treatment

The villagers do not take any medicine or food for general fever, except barley or biscuit for the first two days. For the last ten years, any type of fever is considered as *arhaiya*—a type of influenza which lasts for two and half days and the villagers wait for the temperature to come to the normal. Only after three days they call or contact the local doctor. Sometimes they call the *ojha* (diviner) for a cure by magico-religious practices. For jaundice also, some magico-religious methods are under practice. Sugarcane and radish are used as the indigenous treatment for jaundice because these are easily available and have been suggested by many doctors time and again.

Epidemics like smallpox and cholera were associated with supernatural beliefs. Smallpox is interpreted as an expression of the anger of Goddess Sheetala and use of medicines is strictly prohibited for the whole household. Use of oil and turmeric while cooking the food and taking non-vegetarian dishes are also prohibited during this time. Villagers worship the Goddess Jagadamba (incarnation of Goddess Sheetala) for cure from smallpox and hang neem (margosa) leaves at the door for purification of the air.

Cholera was earlier considered as collective punishment to the whole village for its sins. It was believed that Goddess Durga punishes a whole household, village or locality and it cannot be brought under control. But during fieldwork, it was observed that villagers have developed a confidence that quick medical help can bring the case under control. Awadhiyas and youths of some other *jatis* have the belief that in case of cholera, the doctor should immediately be consulted whereas older people and people of Kahar and Nonia *jatis* still persist the traditional belief. During mid-1975, when maximum cases of snake bites were recorded, the villagers organised a round-the-clock recitation of a holy text to please the God Malanga.

Leprosy is also considered as punishment for one's sins and the Sun God is worshipped for its cure.

So, in these cases, all the three ; prayer of God, services of local specialists, and consultation of block medical officer are found in practice, one after another.

Child Delivery

Child delivery is not considered to be an important event which deserves any special attention. The delivery is attended by *chamain* (a woman of chamar *jati*). The umbilical cord is cut by a new blade. This is a new innovation used instead of a sharp knife. So far, only three women have gone to Muzaffarpur hospital and private nursing homes for delivery. Any complication at the time of delivery is attended by the village quack or by the block medical officer, depending upon the financial position of the household concerned and seriousness of the case.

Family planning

Villagers in general do not give much emphasis to family planning. The villagers' concept about family planning is limited to its message for fewer children. The acceptance of family planning is not universal among the villagers. The cultivators feel that the family size should be small to minimise land division. But they do wish to have atleast two sons and one daughter on the plea that one cannot get salvation unless the funeral fire is lit by a son. The other son is required as a safeguard against accidental death of either. The daughter is also necessary for performing *kanyadan* because he has taken gift of a girl from the society. On the other hand, the poor labourers consider children as a source of income. So, many of them like to have more children, preferably sons, who can contribute to the household economy.

Indigenous methods of abortion are used to control family size. This is done with the help of the *chamain* and quacks who provide herbal medicine for abortion. A few villagers from Awadhiya and Teli *jatis* use '*Nirodh*' (a contraceptive) but they complain that they do not get proper enjoyment with the same and it sometimes gets ruptured. The total number of persons vasectomized till pre-SITE period (August 1975) numbered 13 including males from Awadhiya, Hazam, Kanoo and Dhunia *jatis*. The figure went up to 21 males and 1 female till the termination of the SITE fieldwork (October 1976) which included males from Kahar and Nonia *jatis* also. The only female who has undergone tubectomy is a wife of a government servant who was afraid of government pressure.

Still the old villagers believe that everything is governed by the Almighty and that man should not interfere. They consider abortion a sin.

Health sub-centre

A health sub-centre was opened in the year 1968. It had a full-time trained midwife, and a compounder who were expected to visit the health sub-centre thrice a week. The health sub-centre provides medical facilities to six other neighbouring villages also. This centre is located in a rented two-roomed house with a dilapidated roof and a verandah. The medicines are kept in two cupboards. Construction of a building for the sub-centre was started in 1971 but it has not been completed. It was observed that none of the medical staff were regular and most of the times the midwife did not stay in the village. Doctors too came to the village only once in three months. However, this situation improved when villagers complained against the doctor and the compounder to the block development committee. It led to the transfer of the compounder. Since March 1977 the doctor and the compounder have started visiting the village sub-centre.

The common diseases as observed in the sub-centre are scabies, round worm, eye-sore, asthma, filaria and anemia. Out of these, scabies and round worms are more than 50 per cent. Though the health sub-centre is supposed to undertake the family planning activities, no facility is available for the same. Only one vasectomy was done in January 1976.

Due to the inadequate medical facilities available in the health sub-centre, the sick villagers are attended by quacks. The quacks give allopathic treatment as well as perform minor surgery. They lack knowledge and many times, charge a very high fee. One such quack lives in Ismailpur also.

Services of the state dispensary at Goraul is irregular. The block medical officer is contacted only in the case of emergency, that too by the rich villagers. A prolonged illness is easily suspected as an effect of the evil eye and the diviner is consulted. Villagers want immediate relief from sickness so it has been observed that the quack, the block medical officer and, the diviner, all are consulted simultaneously.

EDUCATION

Since 1971, a lower primary school having three classes was started in the village and was managed by the villagers. These classes were held in Sarvodaya Library. From 1972, the school is being run by the State Education Department.

The one room, one teacher school had (according to the attendance record of July 1976) a total of 61 students on roll. The age of the students ranged from 4 to 13 years. Most of the times, the students remained absent from the classes. The teacher paid attention to four or five students of higher classes to whom he also taught as a private tutor. The school teacher, it was observed, was quite irregular.

In August 1976, the school shifted to a thatched shed. It was done because the education department insisted that the school must have its own building.

The villagers get higher education from High Schools and Colleges located at other places. Low *jati* and scheduled caste people are mostly illiterates. Table 4.1 indicates the educational index of the village and gives an idea about the literacy rate of Ismailpur.

TABLE 4.1 : **Distribution of households according to educational index***

	No. of Households	*Percentage*
Illiterate	79	45.8
Low education	61	35.5
Medium education	25	14.6
High education	7	4.1
Total	172	100.0

* Educational Index is a 'Summated scale'. It was calculated by giving 2 points to literate head of the household and one point to other literate members of the household above 4 years of age. The total score indicate the Educational Index. Low education includes the households having 1 to 3 points whereas medium education includes between 4 to 6, and higher education includes all those having 7 and more points.

URBAN CONTACT

Very few villagers go to the nearby towns ; Mahua, Goraul, or Muzaffarpur for any purchase. More than 65 per cent of the villagers have not visited Muzaffarpur and Hajipur. Four college students of Awadhiya *jati* go to towns occasionally. The Teli households have relatives in Muzaffarpur and other towns whereas the Hazamas have professional contacts from Muzaffarpur, Assam and Darjeeling, where some of them are running hair-cutting saloons. Few Dhunias are rickshaw-pullers at Patna and two Awadhiyas commute between Mahua and the village, as they have business in Mahua. The Mukhia is the only person having good contacts with block as well as district officials.

OTHER AMENITIES

Multi-Purpose Co-operative Society

Multi-Purpose Co-operative Society (MPCS) is the smallest unit at the co-operative department in the state and operates at the panchayat level. The MPCS of Ismailpur has been in existence since 1970. The founder MPCS Secretary was the village Mukhia. But he was forced to resign in 1973 as a result of several complaints against him and his wife has been the Secretary since then.

MPCS in Ismailpur is a one man (Mukhia) operation. The President, the Treasurer and other 141 members in the society hardly know anything about its activities as most of them are illiterate. The MPCS is involved in fertiliser distribution and sale of the fertilizer to the tune of about fifty thousand rupees per year. It is alleged that the MPCS profit goes to the Secretary and this is done in connivance with the block officials and the co-operative bank officials. It is said that the desirous villagers are "debarred" from getting loan despite the fact that rupees fifty-two thousand have been sanctioned to the MPCS for the year 1976-77.

Electrification

The Electrification of the village was done in the year 1964. The Fattehpur transformer supplies power to Ismailpur. Five houses have been electrified so far. Three flour mills and two electric pumps also run on electric power.

Post Office

Ismailpur falls under Sondho postal service range, which is a branch post office (BPO) of the Goraul Post and Telegraph Office. Since 1969, this BPO provides postal facilities to six villages, but its location has changed twice since then. The post office does not have any building of its own and is located in a rented room. It has registered post and money order facilities, whereas telegraphic facilities are available at Goraul.

The post master, belonging to Ismailpur village is responsible for mail distribution to villages falling south of Sondho market whereas the postman distributes mail to the villages falling north of Sondho market. Since the BPO is located near the tri-weekly market, villagers usually receive their letters on market days when they visit the market or the letters are sent through other villagers who visit the market.

Most of the mail is distributed by the Postman while sitting on a bench in the tri-weekly market.

The money order distribution system is in a bad shape. The money order payments are sometimes delayed for several weeks. For example, in the month of February 1976, eight money orders worth about 2,300 rupees were not delivered for about three months. The villagers complained that the Postman charges some 'commission' for delivery of money orders and the minimum commission is one rupee and if it is not paid then it gets delayed.

5

CULTURAL COMMUNICATION

IN THE last two chapters, an attempt was made to describe and analyse the village profile. In this chapter, patterns of cultural communication will be analysed keeping in view that cultural norms govern communication in a stratified rural setting like India. In Chapter 3, it was indicated that social stratification is clearly manifested in the settlement pattern of the village. In this chapter is analysed the settlement pattern in terms of its spatial distribution and the ways in which it relates to communication in the village.

According to Agrawal, "Rural communication is mostly verbal, area and situation specific involving inter-personal communication. . . communication being verbal and expressed through symbols becomes 'culture bound' and codification and decodification of the message is limited to those who are part of and share the culture" (Agrawal 1978 : 73).

One of the main characteristics of cultural communication being verbal, is interpersonal, hence, it becomes a part of larger social networks of household, friends, relatives and *jati* members living in the village or outside the village. Brooks defines inter-personal communication as one ". . .in which persons are engaged directly with each other in overt transmission and reception of messages" (Brooks 1971 : 10).

Cultural communication, being interpersonal and direct, involves various levels of communication within the village and in a cluster of villages where it is interlinked and inter-connected by various kinship, religious, political, and socio-economic obligations and exchanges. The smallest socially viable and spatially definable group in which such communication takes place is the *ghar* or household and the largest being the village and beyond.

Before mapping out the various levels and boundaries in which interpersonal communications take place, the analysis of the process by which a child learns to communicate within the household with its parents, siblings and relatives would permit an understanding of the learning process of communication.

Most of the social scientists working in rural India have indicated that the human knowledge acquisition in most cases, takes place through individual efforts, oral instructions and personal observations (Saraswati 1972). It can be characterized as learning by observation and imitation. In Ismailpur, observations indicate that infants are encouraged to imitate behaviours from a very early age. Parents and relatives encourage an infant to repeat actions, gestures, sounds, and motions enacted and demonstrated by them. While learning a language, again emphasis is laid upon imitation of sounds and gestures. This process continues throughout the life of an individual. Passive acceptance of the method of learning without questioning is an expected role of a good learner.

PATTERNS OF SOCIALIZATION

In the early stage of infancy, the mother and other members of the household 'teach' the baby about different things. One pokes his/her face and laugh so that the baby may repeat the same expression and in this way the baby learns how to laugh. The different sounds are made to attract the attention of the baby if it does not respond to the expression. The baby is asked to pronounce the kinship terms and some of the names of the objects. These terms are repeated and corrected many times before the baby repeates the word correctly. Seeing any new face, when a baby hesitates in going to his/her lap, the mother or other relative encourage the baby by first identifying the relationship, followed by expression of affection or even lure the child by giving some sweets. These acts probably help the baby to remember and respond positively on such situations.

By the time a child is about two to three years, the elders begin instruction about "right things" without giving any reason. The child is checked from eating soil, throwing grain, and going near dangerous places like fire and wells. Invariably in every *jati*, the child is scolded. It creates a sense of fear in the child and inhibits him/her from repeating the undesirable actions. Most of the learning takes place in the form of demonstration and repetitive imitations.

Apart from the *ghar* or household, the other most important learning place, outside the household is a play group which 'teaches' things of general interest. It also provides a forum to exchange new experiences, excitements, and sometimes the so-called secrets of the house. It is quite common to find children playing together outside the house all day, which provides a fairly good amount of time to learn the *jati* differences and community living. It is more so among boys than girls.

In Ismailpur, sex-linked normative behaviour is identified and separated at an early age (generally by four to five years). The sex differences are manifested in role relationships, dress pattern, nature of work and communication boundaries. The boys and girls are strictly kept apart from each other. The activity spheres are so clearly demarcated that boys and girls, to a large extent, are left to wonder about the opposite sex. The girls are forced to maintain distance from boys and clothe themselves, which they learn through observation-imitation. More than the boys, they wonder about themselves. A certain amount of restriction is imposed upon girls and a concept of limited freedom is inculcated among them. In a way, by the time the girls are about seven or eight, they are explicitly told about their different status, vis-a-vis to boys which becomes more and more evident as they grow. Adults of both sexes, regardless of their *jati* and economic position, talk separately on topics related to sexual involvements, experiences and encounters. Problems related to wet dreams, menstruation, and physical weakness are also discussed secretly. However, it is interesting to point out that what is termed as 'private' and 'secret' spreads fast through friendship-networks and soon becomes public. In the process, the message generally gets distorted to the extent that it takes the shape of rumour. This method of message transmission of private and secret matters to public is quite common in Ismailpur.

The socialization process described so far indicates that the instructions flow from the elders to the youngers who are expected to learn it without questioning. Further, the knowledge acquisition comes through imitative behaviour which does not permit reasoning and questioning. However, it helps a high level of accurate knowledge acquisition, necessary for maintaining a continuity in the rural life-style. Within this perspective, four levels of communication, namely, household, *jati*, village and occuptional-level communication are analysed.

HOUSEHOLD COMMUNICATION

The head of the household, in most of the cases, is a male who is either the father, the eldest brother, or the husband. All messages, informations and appeals related to household matters are first conveyed directly or indirectly to the head of the household. In the household, sons, regardless of their age, may directly inform/talk to their fathers whereas daughters talk to their mothers and avoid their fathers, except in Nonia *jati* who are poorest in the village. Irrespective of the nature of talk, persons of equal age group and of the same sex talk among themselves more frequently. Exchange of message between daughter-in-law and father-in-law does not take place, specially in large households. If need arises, the messages are conveyed through those who can talk to the father-in-law. These include mother-in-law, brother-in-law and in some cases husband. In Dhunia, Kahar and Dusadh *jatis*, which are labour households, the father as well as son both discuss economic problems freely. But, the father has a final say in decision-making, particularly in social matters.

Communication within the households also include the exchange of information between husband and wife. The newly-married couples in large households do not talk in the day time, or in front of any elderly member. When they meet in the night, the wife tells about her experiences in the new house and the husband narrates the activities of the day. The talk also includes sex-related topics and most of the time sharing of the bed. Such inhibitions continue for one to five or more years depending upon the social and economic status of the household. For example, in the small cultivator household, the couple talk regarding the things to be done in the field and about the items she should bring in the field. Thus, close working relationships does away with restrictions in the small cultivator households. Couples of rich households do not have to talk about agricultural or economic problems whereas the couples of poor households do have to talk and discuss about it.

Matters related to sex are generally shared with the wife. Sisters-in-law also participate in this kind of talk somewhat openly in almost every *jati*. However, in literate households, sex-related matters are not talked openly. Such talk is indulged in only in the absence of elder relatives.

News of family planning is discussed among couples and in a few cases this matter is also discussed among the wives of two

"My share is 1/16th I harvest"

Agriculture: the source of livelihood

"Where to go tomorrow"?

In gossip group

Cultural Communication

brothers if they belong to the same age group. Sometimes, sisters-in-law also talk about family planning to brothers-in-law. But it is just to create humour. Problems of menstruation and other sex-related matters are strictly discussed among women. First, such matters are discussed with the sisters-in-law or elder sisters or mother, depending upon the availability of these relatives in the household. These relatives may or may not discuss it with others. If discussed with others, the information is bound to spread to a large number of persons within and outside the village through these sources. The information may be filtered, exaggerated or distorted in between, depending upon the nature of the information and interest of the person concerned. Thus, the pattern of communication, in some cases, also takes into account the nature of message and its consequences, if known to others. Individual enmity within the household also leads to exposure of various secret affairs which is generally verbalised to defame the other person. Political matters were found to be discussed only in the Mukhia's household.

The foregoing analysis indicates that the most powerful figure in the household is a male relative who also receives, transmits and exchanges almost every kind of information related to the household. Regardless of *jati* and economic position, he also takes decisions effecting individuals within the household. Any deviation in this normative pattern either leads to weakening of the authority of the head of the household or development of a number of parallel communication sub-systems within the household. This kind of disintegration was observed in the large households.

Expression of love to the children, specially in presence of the elders is avoided thereby accepting the authority of elders not only in collective matters but also in expressing personal feelings. Close observations indicated that spouses do not verbalise their love for each other openly. Such an idea is fairly alien for the villagers. However, jealousy and criticisms are openly and widely expressed.

JATI-LEVEL COMMUNICATION

The *jati*-level communication is an arena of limited but very intense and serious human interaction. Occasions like marriage, death and other functions provide interactive situations in which relatives meet and exchange informations. The set of households invited on such occasions are both relative and non-relative *jati* members. The village barber goes from house to house to extend the marriage invitation. In case of death, relatives themselves go to inform the *jati* members. Even when other *jatis* are invited on these occasions, they do not participate in all the activities like tenth day '*jati* feast'. However, exceptions are made for close friends.

During marriage gathering, women talk about households affairs and also explore possibilities of a match for their son or daughter. They also share gossip and relate events that had taken place in the past. Men exchange occupation-related informations like agriculture work and trade, variety of seed, type of soil, irrigation pattern, crop prospects, marketing situation, and also about the facilities made available to them by different developmental agencies. It is considered polite to share such information.

As a *jati* is spread beyond the village, even on minor occasions, a *jati*-level communication takes place encircling a large spatial area. A similar pattern of intra-*jati* communication can be observed when relatives visit each other, though on a smaller scale.

Familial disputes also provide an occasion for *jati*-level communication in which a large number of *jati* members are involved, specially the near and dear of the grieved parties. Important and respectable *jati* members are invited to settle the dispute in the *jati* panchayat These *jati* panchayats are more active and effective in *jatis* like—Awadhiya, Hazam, Dhunia and Nonia. These panchayat meetings help bring together a *jati* and also in increasing *jati* communication.

Jati-level communication also takes place at the time of collective *jati* festivals both (secular and religious). For example, Awadhiya *jati* celebrates Shivaji centenary every year. In this celebration, a large number of Awadhiya from the region participate. Though no formal announcement is made, the celebration information is passed verbally to *jati* members by the organising committee. During the celebration, efforts are made to bring *jati* members together, to provide a sense of unity and an opportunity to meet, talk and exchange information on a variety of topics.

The individuals in a *jati* also communicate to each other as they have common needs and interest. Women, specially married women, use a variety of human channels to communicate to co-mates and other affinal relatives. Due to lack of education these women send/receive their messages orally through messengers. If the message is very confidential, they arrange a meeting personally. Social norms hamper such meetings. For example, a daughter married within Ismailpur can not be visited by her mother. In such cases, arrangements are made through messengers to meet outside the village by them. Such a communication behaviour is acceptable to the villagers of Ismailpur. As indicated earlier, majority of the *jati*-level communication remain confined to the familial or individual issues.

The foregoing analysis indicates that the *jati*-level communication is an arena of familial and individual interaction. It covers a large area beyond the boundaries of Ismailpur. Exceptions apart, all marriages take place within the *jati* as the marital distance is very small. Hence, on each occasion, regardless of significance when *jati* gatherings take place, relatives exchange information which cover a wide range of personal as well as community/social life.

VILLAGE-LEVEL COMMUNICATION

There are very few topics of common interest either internally generated or reaching through external sources which involve the whole village. The prior information about festival dates is of utmost importance for all who celebrate fairs and festivals. As this information through printed festival calenders are not available to everyone and traditionally the Brahmin is expected to provide, a few individuals contact the Brahmin to get this type of information. They, in turn, pass it on to a few more and this process continues until everybody knows about it. This is true for major festivals like dussehra, deepawali and chhatha. Even the Dhunia who do not celebrate these festivals, know about the dates because of repeated discussions that take place prior to festive days.

Other festivals like Astajam and Saraswati Puja bring all the *jatis* together to organize them. Efforts by a few individuals help bring everyone together who act as prime sources of information. In a formal meeting, which is attended by some of the villagers, the information about the festival dates and the arrangements to be made are verbally passed on to individuals. In this way, it reaches the whole village. When the actual festivals take place, it provides an occasion for face-to-face interaction and communication to many who would not meet otherwise, specially women.

At the formal level village panchayat meets to discuss problems related to village development as a whole, as well as individual problems which could not be settled at kin or *jati*-level. These discussions have very little participation of women. The decisions and discussions of the panchayat are disseminated to other villagers through gossip groups and friends circle.

At another level, certain information of common interest, specially if it happens to be sensational, external but of some special type ; like epidemics, accident, murder and theft, etc., are first brought to the gossip groups and discussed. Most of the active villagers participate in three major gossip groups of the village, located in Eastern Ward, Western Ward and Southern Ward. Similarly, any sensational news about illicit relations are also discussed in the gossip groups. Generally, these gossip groups consist of men. Women from Southern Ward and Dhunia ward also form gossip groups occasionally and discuss information of similar nature.

From the gossip groups the information starts radiating in multiple directions in which the members of the group become informants. Higher the sensational value of the information, the faster is its dissemination.

An analysis of these gossip groups indicate that the membership is voluntary in nature. Physical proximity of individuals and the social relationship determine the membership of the groups which are non-kin oriented. There is a continuous flux in the membership. Within the group, social hierarchy is clearly maintained and elders get precedence over youngers, regardless of *jati* and socio-economic status. It is dominated by one or two knowledgeable individuals who do most of the talking in which others intervene, interject, and question the validity of the information and give opinions. There is no continuity of discussion topics though there is a certain amount of consistency in topical discussions like politics, agriculture, and fairs and festivals.

OCCUPATION-LEVEL COMMUNICATION

As discussed in Chapter 3, agriculture dominates the whole economy of the village. The agricultural work starts with the ploughing of the field. Relatives come to help in this venture and bring information from their villages. The tractor driver who comes to plough the field of rich cultivators and the mechanic who comes to repair the pumping sets are also carriers of information. Tractor drivers carry information particularly related to tractor technology, rate of ploughing, and about other villages where he has served earlier.

For certain agricultural practices like irrigation, the cultivators talk among themselves crossing the boundaries of *jati* and village.

This can be observed any fine morning in gossip groups of the village. People talk on all aspects of village life. This group discussion leads to small group talk in which two or three cultivators, whose fields are adjacent, discuss resources. This is a follow up of communication. The matters about seed and fertilizer are discussed by the village shopkeeper or the outside co-operative storekeeper from where the villagers buy seed and fertilizer. The degree and quality of information the cultivators receive, varies widely from one source to another. The village shopkeeper or fellow cultivator may not give complete information, but if the villagers go to Bhagwanpur or Mahua co-operative depot, they receive information about the varieties of seed and of chemical fertilizers.

The labourers coming for ploughing, weeding and harvesting, both from this village as well as from outside, also act as information carriers. They carry agricultural news from one village to another. The paddy grown in deep water is harvested with the help of boat and the boatmen come from distant places. They also carry agricultural information as well as news of general interest.

The fields provide a suitable place of communication among the labourers coming from different households/*jatis*/wards/villages. Married girls of the labour class talk about their husbands and in-laws while transplanting the paddy. These talks cover many aspects of their personal, village, and economic life. The labourers who have visited other parts of the country talk about their experiences and activities that are going on in the country. While working in the field, labourers also talk to the landowners and learn proper use of fertilizer, transplantation of paddy, or sowing method. In this way, the exchange enriches their knowledge.

The villagers meet various buying agents and talk to them about the market and other news. Important among the agents are the tobacco agents who come to the village from Sismabazar (U.P). They carry along with them, news of people, the market rate of tobacco, and new excise rules for tobacco production. So is the case with Nonia who prepare *khar* (washing soda) and sell it to the agents of Muzaffarpur. The butcher, who comes to buy goats also exchanges information about the market price of goats. During the time of child delivery, the *chamarin* (village midwife of Chamar *jati*). is called for assistance. She gives useful information to the expectant mother.

The artisan and craftsmen come and talk to the villagers. The talks between the mason and the house-owners, the carpenters and the villagers, the blacksmiths and the villagers, the tailors and the villagers and between the brazier and the villagers indicate that it is a free and informal face-to-face exchange of words which starts with occupational intention but also crosses the boundary of occupation and village. Some of these talks are restricted among men and elderly women only.

Except for the young daughters-in-law and girls of the rich villagers, the women of Ismailpur go to the village shops to buy articles of daily use. There, they get a chance to talk and exchange news of mutual interest with the shopkeeper as well as other women of the locality. In some cases, the shopkeeper plays the role of messenger.

Villagers also get a chance to interact with the fishermen who come to Ismailpur for catching fish and also for planting fry in the pond. Through these fishermen, the villagers knew about the different types of fishes, their breeding season, and a bit about its economics. This seasonal interaction is restricted among men and that too with a few rich persons who own or share the pond.

The analysis of occupational communication shows an involvement of a large area and people who share and exchange informations relevant to their day-to-day life. Most of these informations cut across village as well as *jati* boundaries. A majority of these exchanges are verbal and situation specific. At a broader level, it generates a communication network of individuals having diverse occupation but mutual and overlapping interests. In spite of these interests, normative behaviour are strictly adhered to in the communication process.

OTHER COMMUNICATION CHANNELS

Many persons from Ismailpur go to other villages where they receive news from different sources. Many outsiders also come to this village, meet people, and transact different news. Villagers while visiting other villages or nearby marketing centres bring back news from the places they had visited. Sharing these depends upon the nature of information as well as the content of the person's relationships with others.

The weekly village market is the place for exchange of news by women living in different villages around the market area. The visitors as well as the shopkeepers are utilized as message-carriers by these women.

The dancing party from Darbhanga exhibits many traits of Mithila culture through song and dance. The knowledge of religious text is also transmitted by the party. Ismailpur has a snake shaman who is frequently visited by many snake-bitten persons from distant villages for cure. During these visits, they talk to the villagers on different social and cultural issues.

The hawkers selling icecream and biscuit visit many villages of the area and are news-bearers. On query, they share their information. They also act as message-carriers for women whose relatives are living in different villages. The *Madhchhora* (Honey collector from the honey comb) comes from another district. He carries general information on crops and lets it be known to those cultivators who are interested in it.

The regular passers by around Ismailpur village road sometimes act as message carriers. They are used for sending all sorts of messages. But use of these channels depends upon the interpersonal relation of the source and the channel.

Daharia (flood-affected persons) from different districts of Bihar also sometimes visit Ismailpur and inform what has had happened in their area. Drought-affected persons also visit the village sometimes. They identify themselves as Rajasthani. Villagers recognize Rajasthani ladies by their dress. They talk about their state.

Beggars moving within a limited area carry tidings of general welfare as well as specific events of the villages. These beggars generally visit rich households from where they expect alms.

SYMBOLIC COMMUNICATION

Apart from verbal communication, there is a whole host of non-verbal communication that takes place in the village in which a message is conveyed through objects, acts and symbols. To Blumer (1969), human beings act toward things on the basis of the meanings that the things have for them. Thus, any non-verbal communication in which an object or act conveys a message through some culture bond symbols is referred to as 'symbolic communication'. In the present context, these symbolic communications have contextual meanings, though some of them are also understood at broader level. Some of these are discussed on the following lines ;

Wailing Women : It is quite a common scene in Ismailpur to suddenly find women wailing ; in the house, on street, in fairs, or in the field, while hugging and squeezing each other. The nature of wailing and crying differentiates the reason and cause for crying. Meeting of relatives after lapse of time, meeting after the death of a relative, or weeping on the death of someone in the household are some of the reasons for such an act. While crying, if information is exchanged and if crying continues intermittently, it means women relatives met each other after a lapse of time. If crying continues without intermittent talk with loud voice, it certainly denotes a death in the household. For most of the villagers, this is considered to be the natural outburst of women who after marriage go to live in their husband's house.

A Tonsured Man : A tonsured man walking in the village street signifies the loss of his relative.

Cactus at the Door Step : The moment a baby is born, a piece of cactus plant (*Muthia seej*) is placed near the door to let everybody know about the arrival of a new life in the house. It is believed that the cactus will protect the child from evil eyes.

Totaka (spell) : Often a leaf marked with vermilion and few rice grains are kept on the street or in the field to harm some one, to get cured from some continuing disease, to keep the evil spirits away, or for many similar reasons. No villager of Ismailpur will cross the spell knowingly, fearing that the spell will harm him. Further analysis may reveal such more symbols in the village.

The analysis presented so far indicates predominance of verbal communication forming a series of communication boundaries interlinking surrounding areas and their people. In the verbal communication, all the subtleties of the cultural norms are maintained in which flow of information, to a large extent, remains consistent.

6

DEVELOPMENTAL COMMUNICATION

IN THE previous chapter, the existing village communication system has been discussed. Such a communication system "... is self-sustaining and necessary for the maintenance and survival of rural culture" (Agrawal 1978 : 92). In order to have a rapid development or to accelerate the process of development, the need to develop external information is considered essential along with other efforts. It is difficult to imagine that national and economic development can be achieved without the input of external information (Schramm 1964), Rogers (1962). Sachchidananda (1972) and Dube (1976) also hold similar opinions.

Of course, there is an explicit assumption that such an intervention would necessarily disturb the existing structure. There was a clear recognition of this view during the meeting of Latin American Communication Researchers, held in Mexico in 1964. They expressed the view that "overall social, economic, cultural and political factors will also be effected in the effort to develop a society" (Beltran 1976 : 109).

In India, concerted efforts are being made after Independence to use external communication to accelerate the process of rural development. Due emphasis on the role of communication was given while drawing national development policies which is well reflected even in the First Five Year Plan of India (Planning Commission 1952). The creation of the National Extension Service (NES) and the Field Publicity Unit are outcomes of such policies. Both these facilities are expected to operate at the grass-root level.

A sizeable portion of the national budget has been allocated all these years for developmental communication. A defined cadre of developmental agents (both government and non-government) have been inducted to carry out the plans related to rural development. In the village, the Village Level Worker (VLW) symbolizes the commitment of such a massive effort. But, it seems that the scene has changed very little due to a lack of appropriate information and infrastructure facilities to those who need them most—the poor. (All such communication efforts through men or media have been referred to as 'developmental communication' throughout this work.)

For the purpose of analysis, the developmental communication can broadly be classified into (a) mass media, and (b) official channels. In the first category, the information is available for every one in principle. But in the second category, though it is also meant for every one, it is shared among selected persons or target groups. Sometimes, information received from both these channels first passes through an interpersonal network and then spread in a larger social sphere.

MASS MEDIA

Mass media in this context, includes newspaper, radio, cinema and television. Introduction of television being a special event for the villagers of Ismailpur, will be discussed in a separate chapter. Thus, here the analysis will focus on newspaper, radio and the cinema.

Newspaper

Exposure to developmental messages through newspapers or any printed media is minimal in Ismailpur. The villagers do not subscribe to any newspaper. The Mukhia sometime brings newspapers from nearby towns. The resident teachers also sometimes bring newspapers from high school, but it is a rare practice. So, the newspaper information remains confined within the Mukhia or teachers' households. Even then, important informations (mainly about social or political events) are passed on to others who visit them. News is also discussed in the gossip groups.

Radio

Radio is somewhat popular in the village. The village has eight transistor radio sets. Half of them remained inoperative due to lack of repair facilities, owner's disinterest, and the high cost of batteries. A majority of the functioning radio sets are owned by large cultivators (*see* Table 6.1). These sets are mainly used to listen to 'Vividhbharati'—a popular commercial station of All India Radio and Sri Lanka Broadcasting Corporation, from where film songs are broadcast. *Chaupal,* 'a village forum' broadcast from All India Radio, Patna, is another preferred programme of the villagers because the local dialect is used in the broadcast. Even in this programme, folk songs rather than instructional messages are preferred. Group listening of any kind is not common in the village.

Cinema

Very few young literate villagers see cinema when they go to Hajipur, Muzaffarpur, or Patna. Table 6.1 indicates that only 11.0 per cent households have cinema-going members among whom about half are males of medium cultivator households. Very few women have seen cinema. Field Publicity Units are not known to have entered the village boundary.

TABLE 6.1 : **Percentage distribution of households possessing radio or transistor and having cinema-going members by land-holding size**

Landholding Size	*Radio/Transistor*		*Cinema*		*Total*
	Not owning	*Owning*	*Not Going*	*Going*	
Landless	100.0	0.0	100.0	0.0	28.5 (49)*
Small cultivators (up to 5 acres of land)	95.1	4.9	91.3	8.7	37.3 (103)
Medium cultivators (6 to 10 acres of land)	82.4	17.6	47.1	52.9	9.9 (17)
Large cultivators (more than 10 acres)	66.7	33.3	66.7	33.3	1.7 (3)
Total	94.8	5.2	89.0	11.0	100.0 (172)

*Figures in parenthesis indicate the frequency.

In general, mass media has had very little impact on the lives of the villagers of Ismailpur. Whatever little media exposure is observed is utilized by those who are landowners. Table 6.1 shows that mass media availability is directly proportional to the landholding—higher landholding leads to higher mass media availability.

OFFICIAL CHANNELS

The major source of all developmental communications for Ismailpur is the Block Development Office, located at Goraul. The block office communicates to the villagers through various developmental agents working at the village level. The developmental messages are mainly related to agriculture, animal husbandry, health and family planning which have been analysed separately.

Agricultural information

The developmental plans of agriculture are conceived at national level in Delhi and at state level in Patna. In either case, these plans are unfolded at state level by the Director of Agriculture or such state level official through letters or during their regular meetings with District Agriculture Officers. The same procedure is followed by the District Agriculture Officer to inform the Sub-Divisional Agriculture Officers and Block Agriculture Officers. In the block, all developmental programmes related to agriculture are executed by the Block Agriculture Officer (BAO), under the overall supervision and control of Block Development Officer, who is an executive head of all the developmental programmes in the block. The BAO calls a meeting of all the VLWs of the block at a regular interval. In these meetings, VLWs are informed about the new agricultural programmes.

In turn, the VLWs carry the details of the programme to the cultivators of their respective areas. The VLW of Ismailpur is expected to cover villages falling into two adjacent panchayats under his jurisdiction. It is at the VLWs level that the operationalization and execution of a given plan takes place. So, the execution of a programme very much depends upon the perception of the VLW about the programme.

How the VLW would pass the information to the cultivators depends on the content of the information and his relationships with the clients. In the villagers' perception, he carries both 'beneficial' and 'non-beneficial' information. The beneficial information relates to high-yielding variety of seed, cultivators' training programme, and distribution of attractive loans. Such information is conveyed to friends and a few influential and active persons of the village. VLW was very discreet in giving information when Janak seed was to be distributed along with the subsidised agriculture loan for buying fertilizers. He visited the Mukhia and a few other large cultivators for giving this beneficial news. But this information was disseminated to others through the gossip groups. High interest was shown in Janak seed because there was prior information available about it through TV. The information about availability of Janak seed also reached Ismailpur through other villagers who had gone to the block office. The villagers of Ismailpur also received this information through their relative VLWs and Mukhias. Two villagers working as VLWs in other blocks also brought the information.

Some of the non-beneficial information proved to be collection of loans and levy, distribution of target loans (the fixed amount of loan to be distributed by the VLW, failing which he would be marked as an inefficient), and compulsory distribution of seeds. To acquaint the villagers with this news the VLW would visit the concerned houses. He also stops by the flour mills or near gossip centres to inform the villagers about these matters. Printed pamphlets would also be utilized. The notice about co-operative loan recovery was passed through gossip groups. Except for a few negative comments, not much discussion takes place when such information is brought by the VLW to the village.

The beneficial news evokes interest whereas the non-beneficial information generates a sense of indifference. Observations indicate that beneficial information though intensely discussed, remain conspicuous at a whisper level. Efforts are also made to be secretive as reflected in statements like "Do not tell it to the Mukhia otherwise he will not tell me anything in future". The very sight of the VLW in the unimportant places of the village generates suspicion in the minds of small and marginal cultivators. Their first reaction is that he is there for some loan collection and they try to avoid him. If forced to a meeting they listen to the information indifferently and try to move out of his sight without making any commitment.

The visit of block officials in the village is a rare event. Only once did the Block Agriculture Officer (BAO) visit Ismailpur during the entire period of field work. He came to discuss about *kharif* crop with a group of about fifteen 'important' cultivators of Awadhiya and Teli *jatis*.

Multi-Purpose Co-operative Society (MPCS) is supplied with high-yielding varieties of seeds and fertilizers to be distributed among the cultivators, by the department of agriculture. Information coming to MPCS, which being a one-man show, remains confined to the Secretary's kins and friends.

About Animal Husbandry

The Block Animal Husbandry Officer (BAHO) as one of the members of the block development office is expected to provide information relating to animal husbandry. The BAHO is a trained veterinarian having a bachelor's degree. Except on private calls, he seldom visited Ismailpur to treat the cattle or to inoculate or to give any information related to animal husbandry.

When a scheme such as poultry development is introduced by the state government, the BAHO informs about it to a few Mukhias, whom he wants to oblige. The Mukhias carry such information to their villages. In Ismailpur, the Mukhia tries to restrict the information of such schemes to himself or to his relatives and friends.

Concerning health

Among all the developmental efforts, the health effort is most visible in the village. The local health sub-centre located in Southern Ward is the concrete manifestation of this effort. In the health sub-centre of Ismailpur, a female health worker, the compounder, and sometimes the doctor act as the health educators. Observations indicate that the health information needs of the villagers fall short of what have been provided to them by these health workers. An average village is inquisitive about the causes of disease, types of treatment given, and symptoms of various diseases. This characteristic is more prevalent among the literate youth who generally come in contact with the health workers. For women, one of the main sources of health information is the female health worker, popularly called *devijee*, who confines her discussions with young women on topics like menstruation and other gynaecological problems. As a normative behaviour, such discussions are avoided in the presence of older women and the men.

The information related to health is somewhat more open as compared to agriculture and is shared among the villagers. Epidemics like cholera evokes exchange of information between the block health officer and the villagers. On such occasions, vaccinator visits the village and with the help of the Mukhia, the school teacher, and other important villagers, tries to inoculate the entire village. The same procedure is followed on other similar occasions.

For family planning

In the block development office, there is a small family planning unit headed by a doctor designated as family planning officer (FPO) under the control of the block chief medical officer. Family planning mass educators are attached to this unit. It seems that this unit is active only when they are under pressure by the higher officials to fulfil certain targets of family planning operations. On such occasions, the family planning mass educator visits the Mukhia and a few influential persons of the village. He requests them to persuade the villagers to adopt the terminal methods of family planning. He also meets poor low-*jati* people and tries to explain the economic implications of having 'a large family'. He tries to enlist the support of the active youth in his effort. When interviewed, he was found lacking adequate knowledge about the problems arising as a result of overpopulation.

Information regarding a family planning camp is communicated to the villagers through the Mukhia, the VLW, the compounder, and the family planning mass educator. During the fieldwork two family planning camps were organized and one man was vasectomized. In order to do so, the FPO and the other doctors of the camp contacted the Mukhia, teachers, and quacks of the area. The doctors made a request to the Makhia for help and they asked the teachers to co-operate. They also instructed the quacks to bring them cases for operation.

In the Ismailpur health sub-centre a big chart prepared in English provides pictorial information on family planning. Though the villagers do not understand the written words, a few of them quite often ask the compounder about it. On such requests, the compounder was noticed to make faces and talk about 'jelly', 'tablets' and 'condom' in an embarrassed manner.

A poster exhibition was organized by the Family Planning Unit at Sondho market. But the exhibition failed to make any impact on the villagers. One of the reasons was the highly technical diagrams in the poster. The presence of the family planning mass educator was the only clue that these posters related to family planning.

After almost a year of the Emergency, in mid-1976, it was decided by the state and the district authorities to involve all the development workers in a family planning campaign. The VLW, the teachers, the panchayat sewak, and the family planning mass educator were asked to bring two cases per month for operation, failing which their salaries were to be withheld. At once, the block jeeps started dusting the village lanes in search of 'cases'. The teachers were seen talking to the labourers and low-*jati* villagers.

They tried to persuade them for an operation. The block staff took the help of the Mukhia and the Mukhia sometimes tried to coax, cajole, and coerce the villagers for the same which resulted in a sense of terror among the Dhunia and Nonia jatis. They became scared of the jeep and started avoiding the Mukhia as well as the teachers and all government officials. The arrival of a jeep and soft talk of a school teacher was taken as a sure sign of a vasectomy suggestion. The total campaign effect led to a high sense of fear among the villagers.

INCIDENTAL EFFECTS OF DEVELOPMENTAL COMMUNICATION

It is quite a common scene in Ismailpur to observe a congregation of men and children upon arrival of a doctor, the block development officer, veterinarian and many similar development functionaries. A few inquisitive young men take upon themselves the role of 'assistant' and 'guide' to these officials. They follow these persons closely and try to observe their activities and quite often ask several questions. For example, when a doctor is visiting the village, these inquisitive youth would help bring water for washing and boiling syringes. They would also carefully listen to the conversation between the doctor and the patient. They also try to collect the empty medicine phials. At a later date they try to apply these medicines when one reports similar symptoms. It is interesting to note that one such person has become a quack in the process and he is doing pretty well in the village. Some knowledge in the field of cattle disease has also been acquired through the same way.

Sonepur fair

About 60 kilometers from Ismailpur, the Sonepur fair, popularly known as *chhattar* is held annually for a period of one month (December-January). Various departments of the Central and State governments involved in developmental activities use this occasion to inform, educate, and publicise their ongoing developmental programmes. Demonstrations, exhibitions, distribution of printed matters, and film shows are arranged for this purpose.

About 40 per cent male cultivators of Ismailpur generally visit this fair every year for a number of reasons. Important among these are buying and selling of cattle and purchase of domestic articles. They visit developmental stalls and collect printed matter, watch movies, and listen to the demonstrators. While returning home they exchange information among themselves. Back in the village, more

Through street singer

Cultural Communication

"I learn from others
and let others know
......all about health"

The quack

The Television

friends and relatives are involved in the discuss and a gossip group is formed.

In Figure 6.1, an attempt has been made to graphically present the flow of developmental information from various sources in the village. Three major sources identified are, official channels (development agents), mass media, and outside contact (Sonepur fair).

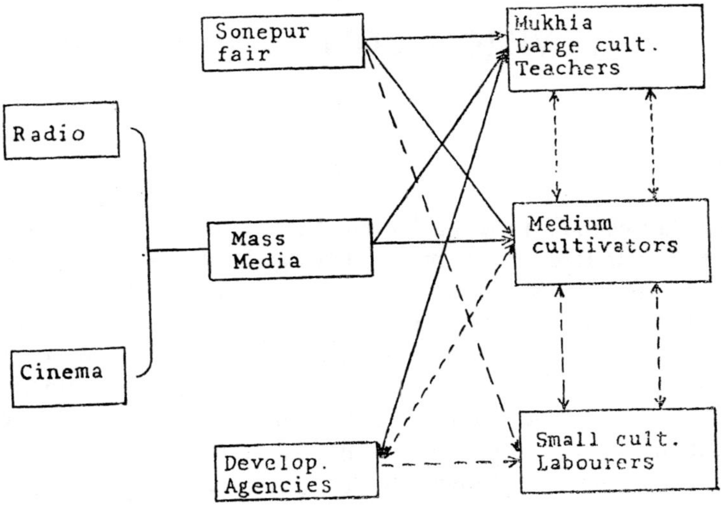

FIG 6.1 : *Flow of Developmental Communication*

The analysis of developmental communication, represents a picture in which few key individuals act as information—mediators or even gate-keepers. The political, economic and intellectual power of these individuals help them to use this system of communication for their advantage at the cost of others. The economic and political powers of key individuals, as analysed in Chapter 3, do not permit any person coming from outside to approach the villagers without going through them. At the same time, such an approach is also convenient, effective and simple for the developmental agents. But this method of communication makes them dependant upon a few. Structurally, this approach of developmental communication, knowingly and unknowingly inhibits developmental agents to meet the target group in most cases. The mass media, though theoretically opened for everyone, do not reach a large section of the villagers because of economic constraints.

7

TELEVISION COMMUNICATION

In the last chapter, the contribution of external sources of information related to development communication was presented. It was observed that the serious efforts of the government for rural development are being utilised by a limited section. Even the mass media have a limited reach. At the moment, there is no single source of information which reaches to the total rural area—due to isolation, high rate of illiteracy, and built-in structural inequality. The introduction of satellite television, as indicated in Chapter 1 was to break some of these barriers and to provide added advantage of picture, sound, motion and emotion.

Earlier efforts to use television for education and development were marked by the urban elites who used it for their entertainment. Dr. Vikram Sarabhai (1969) and his colleague Professor E.V. Chitnis (1976) thought that satellite communication would directly reach rural viewers. According to Pal (1977), satellite broadcasting has a character qualitatively different from any other broadcasting. It allows to broadcast democratically, to all points in the country without discrimination against remote areas which have not been contacted so far. In this way, it is an ideal instrument for the free flow of information. In this framework the responses of the viewers of Ismailpur towards television and television programmes will be examined in the next three chapters. The emphasis in the analysis will be on the instructional programmes.

For the convenience of presentation, the initial responses of television and the factor effecting television viewing will be analysed in this chapter, followed by the analyses of morning and evening transmission separately.

COMING OF SITE

The saga of SITE for the villagers of Ismailpur began when in early August 1974 a biscuit colour jeep having Gujarat number plate of SITE arrived to the village. Except the block education officer, all the co-passengers were young strangers who introduced themselves as members of SITE village-selection-team. They wanted to locate a suitable building where television could be installed. They visited the panchayat building and Fatehpur Middle School and evaluated the technical suitability of these two places. It was a non-event for the villagers, as no one except the Mukhia and a few teachers barely comprehended the purpose of the visit. In order to be nice to the visitors, they expressed their desire to have a television in the village. Very little is known if the Mukhia or other teachers discussed this matter at a later stage.

By January 1975, it became certain that Ismailpur would be one of the 393 SITE villages of Bihar. No one in Ismailpur knew about the selection, though it was communicated to the block development office and the electricity board. At a later stage, the Mukhia came to know about it. One fine morning, when the SITE team arrived to install the antenna, word went around the village. The Mukhia was summoned to open the panchayat building. The children and a few men surrounded the team who were assembling the antenna. After the team had left, many more came to see the "umbrella shaped structure" and that was followed by waves of discussion. Many thought that the Mukhia engineered to get this umbrella installed in the panchayat building like many other good things he had monopolised in the past. This was the first indication that television was considered as something good. A new nomenclature to this structure was given—*chhatta* (umbrella). Many used to stop by in front of the antenna and wonderd as to how the picture would appear in it. By the time the researcher arrived in the field, in the first week of March 1975, sporadic discussions continued about possible reasons for installing television in Ismailpur and its future implications. Many thought that the television was meant for propaganda to help win elections and to counter attack the serious anti-government agitation led by Jai Prakash Narayan at that time. Others were worried that additional taxes would be imposed. By May 1975, the television set was delivered and in early June, the panchayat building was electrified under the personal supervision of Sub-Divisional

Officer, Electricity. By the time the television became operational, the school teacher and the panchayat sewak (attendant) were given charge of its operation.

In Ismailpur, the television was installed independent of any political or administrative interference, either at the block or the state level. For the first time in the village history, a 'government' sponsored plan was executed so quickly. This event led many to believe that projects of Delhi (central government) are executed more efficiently and expeditiously as compared to Patna (state government). Further, it gave credibility to all those who were connected with television.

SITE BEGINS

With the installation of the antenna, people eagerly awaited the starting date of the television programmes. The block officials, SITE technicians, locally educated persons, newspapers, and the resident researcher gave assurance that 'it would start from 1 August, 1975'.

On this afternoon many people from neighbouring villages rushed to Ismailpur because five other television sets installed in villages around Ismailpur were not functioning. Many students missed their school and gathered around the television centre. Girls came in groups wearing colourful dresses. By 5.30 p.m. children had already assembled. Carpets were arranged for block officials and other important invitees. At 6.00 p.m. there were more than 300 persons. But due to sudden heavy rain the viewers had to shift indoors. The prime place in the room was reserved for important invitees. The room became overcrowded with nearly 150 persons inside. The television set was inaugurated by the block development officer (BDO). The first television broadcast was the Prime Minister's message.

This started the beginning of a year-long community television viewing in Ismailpur. Ismailpur gained special status as it was selected for the SITE Social Evaluation Study. In spite of having 13 television sets under the jurisdiction of this block, the BDO's coming to this village for the inauguration added further laurels. A descriptive analysis of an evening of television viewing, after the novelty effect was over, is presented here.

Characteristic of the viewers and non-viewers

The analysis of viewers, characteristics is based on a door-to-door enquiry made twice during the field work. It was made once in the month of January, 1976 and the second time immediately after SITE in August 1976. Table 7.1 provides the distribution of viewers by age and sex which were 171 in number. Little over one quarter of the total viewers were females. Whereas more than 72 per cent were males. For a number of reasons as indicated earlier, women could not view TV as much as men could. Among females, the largest group of viewers belong to the 5—14 years age group, mostly unmarried girls of the village, followed by slightly older women in the age group of 25—34 years. On the contrary, among males, the youth between 15 to 24 years of age dominated the viewers group. Typically the young unmarried women were restricted from viewing television. Table 7.2 shows that more than 53 per cent viewers are illiterate in which the housewives are largest in number. Among the viewers there are 18.7 per cent educated to primary level and 26.3 per cent till Secondary education.

TABLE 7.1 : **Percentage distribution of the viewers according to sex by age groups**

Age group	*Sex*		*Total*
	Male	*Female*	
5 to 14 years	16.2	34.0	21.1
15 to 24 years	30.6	12.8	25.7
25 to 34 years	22.6	25.5	23.4
35 to 44 years	15.3	12.8	14.6
45 to 54 years	9.7	10.6	9.9
55 years and above	5.6	4.3	5.3
Total	72.5	27.5	100.0

Sample size 171

There were only 1.8 per cent or three post-secondary educated viewers in which one viewer was a businessman whereas to others were professionals. Table 7.2 shows that educated viewers are distributed evenly in all categories of occupations except housewives where none of them attained secondary education.

The picture that emerges from the above analysis is that an average television viewer in Ismailpur was an illiterate male youth involved in agriculture for his livelihood.

An analysis of 'potential television viewers' (all above four years of age) in Table 7.3 indicates that 45.2 per cent are males and 54.8

TABLE 7.2 : **Percentage distribution of the viewers according to education by occupation**

Occupation	*Education*				*Total*
	Illiterate	*Primary*	*Secondary*	*Post Secondary*	
Cultivation	23.1	31.3	44.5	0.0	29.8
Labour	24.2	3.1	4.4	0.0	14.6
Business	5.5	9.4	4.4	33.3	6.4
Professional employment	1.1	0.0	2.2	66.7	2.3
Student	0.0	46.8	42.3	0.0	19.9
Housewife	35.1	9.4	0.0	0.0	20.6
No work	11.0	0.0	2.2	0.0	6.4
Total	53.2	18.7	26.3	1.8	100.0

TABLE 7.3 : **Percentage distribution of the non-viewers according to sex by age group**

Age Group	*Sex*		*Total*
	Male	*Female*	
5 to 14 years	45.8	33.8	39.2
15 to 24 years	13.3	16.1	14.8
25 to 34 years	13.0	14.8	14.0
35 to 44 years	11.8	11.8	11.8
45 to 54 years	6.8	8.2	7.6
55 years and above	9.3	15.3	12.6
Total	45.2	54.8	100.0
		Sample size	714

per cent are females. Most of them are in the age group of 4 to 14 years. The rest of them are almost equally distributed among both the sexes. The analysis of non-viewers' educational qualification shows that, in proportion to the village literacy, approximately 75 per cent of the non-viewers are illiterates whereas the percentage of illiterate viewers are only 53 per cent. The comparison highlights the higher proportion of the secondary educated viewers (26.3%) as compared to non-viewers (9.2%). Among the primary and post-secondary viewers and non-viewers the difference is not marginal.

Table 7.4 shows that among the non-viewers 32.9 per cent are housewives followed by 22.8 per cent of them having no work. The reason may be that the persons above the age of 55 years do not have any work responsibility, particularly in the cultivators' households. Hence 12.6 per cent of that age group is of non-viewers (*see* Table 7.4). Comparatively, there are more cultivators who are viewers than non-viewers. Only 8.1 per cent of the village population is engaged in business and most of them are from Hazamtoli. Hence, the percentage of businessman viewers are more than non-viewers. These non-viewers lived in Northern Ward and could not come to view television regularly due to long distance.

TABLE 7.4 : **Percentage distribution of the non-viewers according to education by occupation**

Occupation	*Education*				*Total*
	Illiterate	*Primary*	*Secondary*	*Post Secondary*	
Cultivation	10.4	9.9	36.4	22.2	12.9
Labour	16.4	4.0	3.0	0.0	13.2
Business	0.9	2.0	6.1	0.0	1.5
Professional employment	0.2	1.0	3.0	66.7	1.4
Student	0.0	73.2	51.5	11.1	15.3
Housewife	42.4	6.9	0.0	0.0	32.9
No work	29.7	3.0	0.0	0.0	22.8
Total	75.4	14.1	9.2	1.3	100.0

Attendance and audience size

The attendance of television viewers varied throughout the experimental year. For the first two months, the attendance ranged between 500 and 800. However, gradually the attendance declined. The lowest attendance of 15 to 20 viewers was observed in the months of December 1975 and January 1976 (*see* Fig. 7.1). By November 1975, it was observed that most of the viewers started losing interest as it was no more a novelty. Some viewers also began to comment on the deteriorating quality of entertainment programmes. Guardians of the students had a complaint that their wards did not read in the night and came to watch television. Just to check their children, they also stopped coming. Many villagers found television viewing unimportant and lost their interest. From October 1975 onward television sets in the five neighbouring villages were repaired thereby leading to further reduction in the viewers' size. Rains and frequent power failure were important factors affecting the viewers' size. From November 1975 to January 1976 paddy harvesting and severe cold further adversely affected the viewer size.

Figure 7.1 shows a gradual increase in attendance after February 1976. It was due to slack agricultural period and warmer weather. In

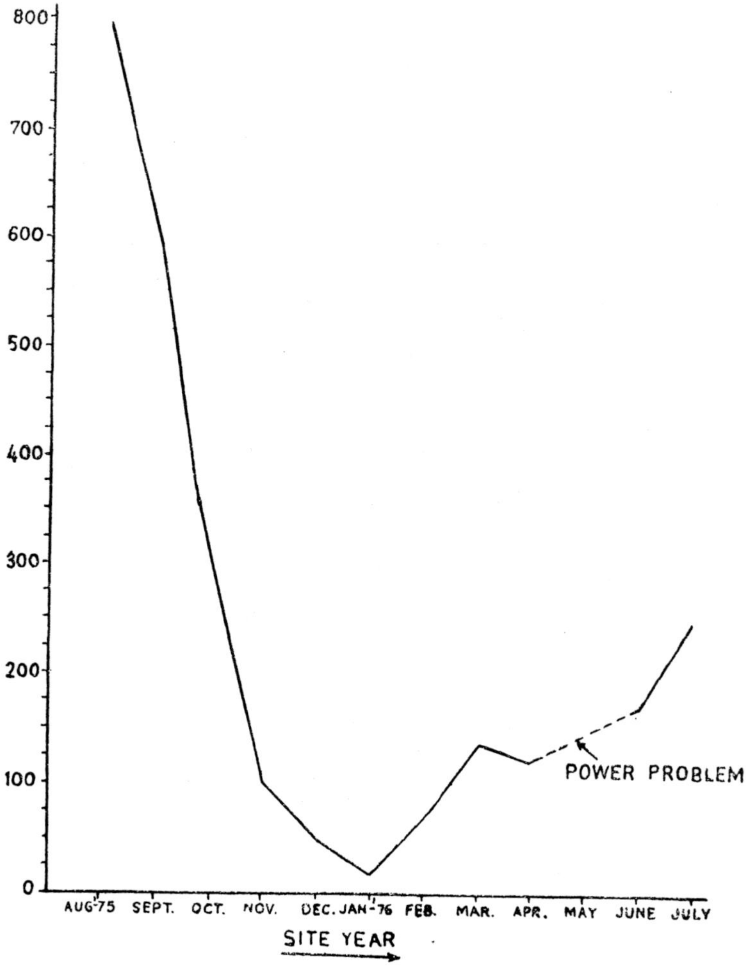

FIG. 7.1 : *Average of viewers' attendance by months Ismailpur (Bihar)*

the last one and a half months—June and July 1976—again there was an increase in viewer attendance. It was because the viewers came to know that the TV would be withdrawn after 31 July, 1976

Apart from these, a number of situational factors also affected the interest of the villagers in television viewing. Important among these were the performance of drama, dance, round-the-clock recitation of religious texts and major panchayat meetings usual at this time of the year. On the occasion of marriages in the village, the viewer number also reduced because many villagers remained busy in managing the feast.

The Sunday television programmes attracted a large number of viewers compared to other days in the week. The reason, as told by them, was that the programmes on Sunday were more entertaining. Particularly the fourth Sunday of the month when a movie, a production of the Children's Film Society was usually shown became an attraction for them.

Core viewers

All together there were five male and two female core viewers. They were all from Awadhiya *jati*, living in the ward nearest to the television centre. The two female viewers were the Mukhia's wife and the daughter. They did not have any work responsibility in the evening. Out of five male viewers, two were heads of the household in the age group of 25 to 34 years having about two acres of land. The other two were unemployed non-matric youths of 20 and 22 years and belonged to well-to-do households and were without any responsibilities. The fifth one was an illiterate unemployed 20 years old youth who had nothing to do in the house. So he came to watch.

The reasons for television viewing differed for these persons. But all of them liked viewing television. For the youth it was a good friend who entertained them. For the cultivators it provided information and for the unemployed it kept them busy in the evening. For women, it kept them out off the house work.

Language of the programmes

Ismailpur is a Bajjika-speaking village, as indicated in Chapter 3. Except a few literate ones, who can speak and understand Hindi, a majority of the viewers, especially the women, found it difficult to comprehend the Hindi programmes. The problem of comprehension became further aggravated even for the 18.7 per cent who were educated to the primary levels when chaste Hindi was used by the com-comperes, experts and subject-matter specialists. Even in discussion programmes where cultivators participated the use of technical terms were confusing to the viewers. One of the major complaint was the fast speech delivery. Similarly, the local equivalents of the agricultural implements were not spelled out by the experts and the viewers found it difficult to comprehend. It is precisely because of these two reasons that programmes like *Yogabhyas* and *Gharelu Ilaj* became very popular as the experts spoke very slowly and as far as possible used popularly known terms. This problem, however, did not exist in the case of dances and songs which were enjoyed by the viewers regardless of language, though they preferred such programmes in Bajjika, Bhojpuri and Maithili.

Working of television set

SITE Television Performance Report by Space Applications Centre (Bhatia 1977) observes that during SITE the overall availability of sets in all the six clusters, after attaining a steady state was 84 per cent. Of the 16 per cent non-functioning sets about 10 per cent were not functioning due to set failure and 6 per cent were not functioning due to electricity failure. The non-functioning of sets due to electricity failure in Bihar was 15.5 per cent.

In Ismailpur, the television functioned well. There was a loss of only nine days due to breakdown of the set during the entire year. The major factor affecting its functioning was power supply which remained irregular throughout the year. Once, the transformer of Ismailpur got burnt out and for replacing the same it took almost 75 days.

Low voltage was another problem leading to video distortion. The presence of flour mills (with power consumption) in the village also affected the proper functioning of the set. At least fifteen times the village youth requested and pressed upon the mill owners not to run the mill during television showing hours.

Role and reaction of custodians

There were two custodians appointed for the operation of the television in Ismailpur. One custodian was the panchayat sewak (attendant) who operated the television during the evening transmission and the other was the teacher, from the local Lower Primary School who operated the television during morning transmission. Ideally, the panchayat attendant was the "first custodian" who was supposed to supervise at both times. Both were, however, supplied with a key to the television room.

The panchayat attendant lived in his village, about five kilometers north-east to Ismailpur. But after taking the responsibility of custodianship he started living in the panchayat building. He is a 40-year old man of Dusadh *jati*. He is a matriculate and has been working for the last three years. He is the head of his household having a wife, a son, and a land-holding of nearly one acre. He collects land revenue and maintains all the panchayat records.

Right from 5.30 p.m. viewers start looking for him to make sure that the room will be opened in time. It is also not uncommon to see him rushing towards the television centre on his bicycle to put the television in the verandah. He adjusts his watch, with the time shown on television.

The user teacher is a 30-year old matriculate and is also of Dusadh *jati*. He is a resident of another village, 14 km. away from Ismailpur. He lives in an adjacent village Majhia and visits his native village on holidays and Sundays. He teaches the students of the household in return for boarding and lodging. From home he would go to school at about 10.45 a.m. and collects the students to go to the television centre. After the television transmission is over, he leads the students back to the school.

In the beginning, both custodians worked regularly but in latter phase, the panchayat attendant was not regular in his duty and remained absent. On such occasions he gave the key of the room to a villager who would operate the television. The main reasons of his absence during the programme were :

1. He was physically a weak man and had to take rest many times.
2. In his stay at the village he took his meals at the Mukhia's house and they, considering him as an extra burden, instigated him to go home.
3. In the beginning people were curious about television and pressurised him to be regular.
4. He was the man directly under the charge of the Mukhia. He had to work according to the Mukhia's instructions and that of block officials. So, sometimes, due to pressure of work he was not able to return in time and open the room in the middle of the programmes.

The second custodian, user-teacher tried his best to be regular in switching the television in time. He rarely gave any instruction or explained any programme to the children. When the programme was over he would put back the television. At least thrice in a month no programme was shown to the students when he went home or went to draw salary or went to the block office for official or personal work.

Both custodians felt that custodianship was imposed on them. They were given such a responsibility without their consent and felt restricted in movement.

The first honorarium to the custodians was paid in the month of February 1976 in a lump sum for the past six months. The next six months honorarium was not paid until September 1976. So that incentive did not work.

The following chapters will limit discussion on the instructional topics—both related to SITE objectives and other than SITE objectives which were the communications directly concerning rural development.

8

TELEVISION AND EDUCATION

TELEVISION has been used by many countries for supplementing school education for various age groups. Researched on its impact and various related aspects have also been highlighted in countries like Australia, Canada, Korea, New Guinea, Sweden, UK and USA (Bates 1977). According to Maccoby (1963 and 1969) television could shape children's attitude and beliefs. Lesser (1974) thought that television could benefit children directly rather than harm them. Belson (1977) found that television increased quite appreciably the level of American boys' involvement in violent behaviour without any change in their conscious attitudes towards violence as a result of television viewing. Searle (1977) holds the opinion that children have predominantly visual memories which might suggest television to be particularly important as an educational tool. Coldevin (1977) indicates that television has appreciably altered the fundamental attitude among the students and the changes are directly proportional to television exposure.

The philosophy of education was conceived because science is everywhere, and the immediate environment can be questioned, understood, explained and manipulated by children by using the scientific method more effectively than mere transfer of information (Aghi 1977 : 2).

The impact of the SITE morning transmission was evaluated by some of the researchers. Important among them are Aghi (1977), Bhaskaran and Patel (1977) and Shukla and Kumar (1977). To Aghi, the television has assisted the students in forming an attitude towards science. Bhaskaran and Patel conclude that, in general the entertainment programmes were comprehended better than the general science and social studies programmes. Shukla and Kumar points out that the school children did not learn from the content of science education programme.

In the light of these discussions the present chapter will try to describe different aspects of the morning transmission, meant for school children of 5—12 years of age and its impact on the students of Ismailpur. It will also deal with the teacher's training programme in which the television was used as one of the media.

RURAL EDUCATION IN BIHAR

The rural education in Bihar is governed by the Department of Education, Government of Bihar. This department functions with its units at the district, sub-division, and block level. At the block level, the overall supervision and administration of education is looked after by the block education extension officer. The appointments and transfers of the teachers are governed by the district education officer.

The opening of a school in a particular village takes place in two ways ; (a) the district education officer, on the instruction of the directorate of education, issues the sanction of the school to a concerned block. The block education extension officer then decides where to open the school and sends back his recommendation to the district education officer for final approval, and (b) the villagers make their representation to the block office and the block education extension officer forwards the paper putting his recommendations to the district education officer. In case of a positive response from the district education officer, the block extension education officer takes the necessary action to open the school.

Origin of the school in Ismailpur

The history of the Lower Primary School in Ismailpur goes back to the mid-sixties when a villager, working as a school teacher in Fatehpur Middle School initiated a school in Ismailpur. He wanted to open a girl's school. After several years of running around, finally in the year of 1970, a Lower Primary School was approved for this village. He wanted to have the school located in Hazamtoli. According to him this place was centrally located. But the Mukhia of Ismailpur did not like the location of the school. He approached the block office and got the approval in abeyance on the plea that sufficient number of girls were not available. In the meantime, the Mukhia built a semi-*kutchha* shade near his house and appointed a teacher on his own and started the school. Due to village politics the residents other than those of Southern Ward did not send their children to this school. Even in the Southern Ward those who were anti-Mukhia or who had already enrolled their children in another school did not send their children to this school ; mainly because of the temporary nature of this school.

The anti-Mukhia group also did not rest on their laurels. They, with their contacts in the district education office were able to influence. the decision. So, the Mukhia's school was not officially approved. The anti-Mukhia group also started a voluntary school in the Sarvodaya Library building located in Western Ward and the classes were managed by two unemployed educated youth. In the year 1972, a Lower Primary School for boys was again sanctioned and recognition was given to this school. The school continues to run in the Sarvodaya Library building. The school was initially started with 17 students. According to the attendance register of July 1976 the total number of students enrolled were 61. The age of the students varied from 4 years to 13 years. In the month of August 1976, the school was shifted under a thatched shade as there was technical objection from the Department of Education that the school must have its own building.

The non-functional Sarvodaya Library Building has one room of 2.5×2.5 m. a verandah of 2.5×4 m. The room is used for keeping the attendance register, a table and two chairs. The verandah is used as the class room. The students of all the three classes of grade one, two and three sit together and a single teacher teaches them together. Generally, the absenteeism rate is very high in the school. The teacher is fond of a few students whom he teaches privately also at home.

The foregoing analysis of the origin and the functioning of the school indicates that even education is ridden with factional politics of the village. The felt need of having a school for all the children of the village fell prey to the Mukhia and anti-Mukhia forces to have locational advantage of the school.

MORNING TRANSMISSION

The $22\frac{1}{2}$ minutes Hindi programme for Bihar* (from $11.07\frac{1}{2}$ to 11.30 hours) covered different topics. The topicwise distribution is presented in Table 8.1

* The same programmes were telecast for Rajasthan and Madhya Pradesh Schools.

TABLE 8.1 : **Estimated topicwise distribution of morning transmission**

Topic	*Percentage*
Science Programme	54
Health and Nutrition	8
Entertainment	13
National Awareness	9
Handicraft	3
Social & Religious programmes	4
Biographies of great men	4
Emergency	2
Others	3
Total	100

The major area of concentrated programming was science, followed by entertainment, travel around India, and health and nutrition, in that order. There was a small amount of coverage on the biographies of great persons. A lecture coupled with demonstration was the most frequently used single form of presentation in the morning transmission. This was followed by films, drama and group discussions. On an average two programmes were telecast every morning. The majority of programmes ranged from 6 to 15 minutes duration.

Based on the teacher's log book and the researcher's own notes, it is estimated that on an average out of six days in a week, the students of Ismailpur could view television for about three days, thereby, indicating that about half of the programmes were viewed.

Before analysing how viewers responded to the television programmes it would by important to understand the contents of the television programmes.*

* This question assumes a great importance as it was well stablished very early that in the communication process a central position is occupied by the content (Berelson 1952). In case of television, any particular type of content is not inherent. It is the use to which television is put by the planner. While the content involve a decision-making, it also reflects as to what the programme wishes to convey. The content also helps to define as to what should be the desired effect. The samples script in English is taken from earlier report (*see* Mody and Sarupriya).

Keeping this view in mind, in the context of SITE, several attempts were made to analyse the content of the progrmmes. Notable among them are Mody and Sarupriya (1977), and Bhaskaran and Patel (1977).

EFFECTS OF TELEVISION

The morning programme was planned for the students of 5 to 12 years of age covering first to fifth grades (*see* Chapter 1). As Ismailpur Lower Primary School was up to grade three, in the beginning it was thought that students from the Fattehpur Middle School should also be asked to view television. A similar proposal was also made for the students of Majhia Lower Primary School.

For first few days, the students from Majhia Lower Primary School came to view the programme regularly. So was the case with the students of Fattehpur Middle School who came in gradewise rotation. After two weeks the Majhia Lower Primary School students stopped coming and after about one month the Fattehpur Middle School students also discontinued this practice. The main reason was the distance of the television centre from the schools. The television centre was approximately 600 m. from Majhia Lower Primary School and 700 m. from Fattehpur Middle School. Teachers of Fattehpur school has another grievance as why was this television set not provided to the middle school. Even though the BEEO wanted to continue this exercise, this could not happen and the total programme was viewed only by the students of 1 to 3 grades who were, according to the researcher's observation, not more than 35 on any given date which included a few non-student children and sometimes adult viewers of the village.

COMPREHENSION AND KNOWLEDGE GAIN

The science programmes were not comprehended by the students as they were young students of first, second and third grades. Not only the students, but sometimes even the teacher did not comprehend some of the science programmes. For example, a demonstration of an electric circuit and lever system was not comprehended by the teacher. Only the students of second and third standards understood the instructions given by the "television teacher" in Hindi. A few students also tried to sketch the drawings shown on television. They picked up the words—*namaste* (a word of greeting), *prathamik Siksha* (primary education), and *samapt* (the end).

In general, the programme comprehension was poor among younger students, particularly for science programmes as indicated. The programmes on "national awareness" and biographies of great men could not be followed by them. They also could not comprehend programmes relating to 'National Emergency'. From health and nutrition programmes they could only grasp that one should take bath daily and keep the surroundings clean. But what is a bacteria and how it affects health was beyond their comprehension. On the other hand, the dance programmes were viewed with attention. Children enjoyed the songs and dances. Dances of non-Hindi areas were also liked.

Pictures of various natural phenomena and objects, to some extent, were liked. Not the ideas or content but only the associated pictures were liked as they see many such things in their village like birds, animals and vegetables. Thus, the children were happy to see ponds, trees, birds, and animals on the screen which they usually see in their day-to-day life. They tried to recognize the objects and immediately announced the name. There was a competition among the children for this.

The analysis presented so far covered the student viewers of the morning transmission. In the morning transmission during Dussehra holidays (October 1975) and summer holidays (July 1976) the morning television time was utilised to train science education teachers. One of these two training programmes was held in Ismailpur. The analysis of the training programme is presented in the following pages.

TEACHERS' TRAINING PROGRAMME

The Multi-Media Package training programme for the teachers was organized in collaboration with the centre for Educational Technology, National Council of Educational Research and Training, Delhi from 16 to 30 October 1975. It consisted of using the printed media, interpersonal discussion, radio and television, and actual experimentation. The training was conducted twice—once in the month of October 1975 and the other in the month of July 1976. The motive for this training was to train the village school teachers in teaching science through a minimum requirement of apparatus and the use of locally available materials. It was also recommended that many good experiments of science can be quoted from natural phenomena.

Ismailpur was the venue for the first training while it was exempted for the second programme. There were ten trainees and one monitor teacher involved in it. Some of the teachers selected from each block had been given training by the State Education Department at Muzaffarpur and were used as monitor teachers.

The names of the teacher for this training was recommended by the block authorities. When the news of the training programme reached the teachers and the villagers, from block headqarters, it was a surprise to all that the teachers would be tought through television. Not only the illiterate villagers and the students but the teachers themselves were curious to know more about this. There was a rumour that these teachers would also be given the type of training as the custodians were given for operating the sets. The user teacher of Ismailpur was one among the trainees.

The training programme started on 16 October 1975 with a little confusion as the user-teacher could not come in time to open the room, the list of participants was not made available to the monitor teacher and the programme literature for the trainees were not supplied for first three days.

The trainee teachers were supposed to read the programme literature and get acquainted with the subject matter to be telecast. Then there was a programme to be followed by a post-telecast discussion among the participants. They were also supposed to prepare a post-telecast report for each programme. The same process was to be repeated with a special All India Radio broadcast in the afternoon. But this practice was hardly followed and the chorum of eleven was never complete.

When they came into the television room they exchanged greetings and discussed the news they brought with them. They watched the Hindi telecast and then based on a very brief discussion, prepared the post-telecast report. After lunch and tea, they were busy gossiping till 2.20 p.m. After that the special radio broadcast was scheduled for their training course. After the broadcast they prepared a post-broadcast report and the day's business was over. Inspite of some suggestions from the trainees side the experiments were never conducted in classroom situations.

Some villagers also came to see Hindi programmes as well as to see the activities of the teachers. Twice the BEEO himself participated in the programme but his instruction to be attentive did not yield any result. Most of the participants seemed not interested for various reasons :

(a) Some trainees had poor understanding level and they could not fully comprehend the theme of the programme.
(b) The old teachers who were about to retire were not interested in learning the new skills at their last phase of professional careers.
(c) The *jati* and religious feelings and the departmental politics prevented a team spirit.
(d) They were not sure about the payments of their special allowance as the remuneration of custodians had not been paid so far.

A few comments made by the participants were :

(a) The situation in which the television teacher deals is different from the way we deal—the ratio of teacher and student, the pay scale, the fund and resources available.
(b) The standard of teaching by television is much higher than the local standard.
(c) If the teacher takes the boys outside the school to observe the natural phenomenon, the guardians in general will object.
(d) How can a teacher press upon a student about washing clothes when he knows the financial position of their guardians makes it impossible, at least for some of them.

At the rural school learning is done through repetition and seldom do all enrolled children come regularly to school. Even the television could not attract more than 35 students out of 61 enrolled in the school (*see* Chapter 4). These children were also not fortunate to view the programmes for more than half of the telecast days.

Science education programmes which constituted the bulk of the telecast could not be comprehended by the Lower Primary School students. This finding is similar to what others have found elsewhere. Recently, the researchers of Children's Television Workshop (CTW) has offered a plausible explanation—it was found in USA that the science concept formation takes place after 9 years of age in a child. If with the better educational facilities in USA, the children are unable to comprehend science programmes in this age group, in all probabilities the Ismailpur children would not be able to comprehend the science programmes. The other programmes in which visual identification was higher than concept learning were more easily comprehended.

9

DEVELOPMENTAL INSTRUCTION

THE PLANNING of SITE in India was based on the experiences gained during a pilot project, *Krishi Darshan*, as well as the studies conducted by Unesco with the tele clubs in the villages of France and Japan. Both in the Japaneese and Indian studies it was suggested that social, cultural and educational programmes should contain an element of entertainment and recreation that can produce a strong emotional effect (Borra 1970).

The selection of programmes for SITE was based on the suggestions made by the experts in the concerned user ministries—both at the Centre as well as at the State. A close liaison was established with the ministries of agriculture, health, family planning and education. Some programme ideas were also drawn from the audience profile need assessment study conducted in various clusters. However, due to lack of time and the load of work, it was not possible to hold a series of meetings with the experts and pre-test all television programmes. A considerable thought was also given on the regional as well as seasonal variations of the agricultural topics being common for Bihar, Madhya Pradesh and Rajasthan as referred in Chapter 1. For field demonstration, the farms and demonstration plots of the Indian Agricultural Research Institute, and Agricultural Universities were used. Similarly, the programmes related to health were shot in different health centres around the Base Production Unit—Delhi and other clusters. Experts were called to the studio for talks and discussions.

The evening telecast can broadly be categorised into (a) programmes on agriculture ; animal husbandry ; health, hygiene and nutrition ; and family planning—referred to as 'hardcore' programmes, (b) instructional programmes on other than the above-mentioned SITE objective areas—referred to as 'softcore' programmes, and

(c) entertainment programmes. Table 9.1 shows that there was 31.1 per cent hardcore programmes (11.9 per cent agriculture ; 3.1 per cent animal husbandry ; 11.4 per cent health, hygiene and nutrition ; and 4.8 per cent family planning). The softcore programme includes 14.8 per cent instructional programmes, other than SITE objectives. Entertainment has a lion share of the total programme (54.1 %).

TABLE 9.1 : **Programme content by broad categories**

Programme Category		*Total Number of Programmes*	*Percentage*
Hardcore			
Agriculture		204	11.9
Animal Husbandry		53	3.1
Family Planning		81	4.7
Health, Hygiene and Nutrition		194	11.4
Softcore			
Instructional Programmes (other than SITE objectives)		253	14.8
Entertainment			
Entertainment Programmes		924	54.1
	Total	1,709	100.0

HARDCORE PROGRAMME ANALYSIS

Agriculture

From among 532 hardcore programmes, 204 or about two-fifth programmes were devoted to agriculture. Table 9.2 provides distribution of agricultural programmes by topic and format. In almost 34 per cent of the programmes, interview, discussion, lecture and talk formats were used whereas 31.4 per cent programmes were produced in field demonstration format, followed by a documentary, graphic, and still. Table 9.2 shows that a variety of topics were covered. Important among them were, use of fertilizer ; use of pesticides and insecticides ; irrigation and after care.

Viewers' preference and adoption behaviour

The cultivators appreciated the programmes related to high-yielding variety of wheat seed and were eager to know more about the high-yielding varieties of potato and sugercane seeds. The television programmes related to after-care of vegetable were criticized. To them,

TABLE 9.2 : **Agricultural programmes by topic and format**

Topic	Format				Total
	Interview Discussion Lecture	*Field Demon-stration*	*Documentary*	*Graphics, Stills*	
HYV of seeds and seed treatment	13.2	1.6	8.2		7.3
Fertilizer	10.1	21.9	4.9		11.8
Pesticides, insecticides and plant protection	15.9	6.2	11.5	50.0	13.2
Irrigation and after care	7.2	17.2	13.1	10.0	12.2
Soil/water testing	10.1	4.7	1.6		5.4
Field preparation	4.3	21.9	3.3		9.3
Sowing method/ Harvesting/storage	11.6	4.7	13.1		9.3
Mechanised agriculture		3.1	11.5		4.4
Vegetable growing	7.2	7.8	11.5	30.0	9.8
Others	20.3	10.9	21.3	10.0	17.3
Total	33.8	31.4	29.9	4.9	100.0 (204)

it was impossible to save the crop from frost by the method suggested/demonstrated on television. They also did not like the programme on cotton plantation which is not grown in Ismailpur. But, they wanted to view programmes on tobacco cultivation. Unfortunately, due to power failure the viewers could not see tobacco related programmes though these were telecast twice.

The cultivators of Ismailpur liked programmes in which field demonstration formate were followed. It involved actual field shots. But they did not like the programmes in lecture, talk, and discussion formate as the villagers believed that by giving lecture and talk one is merely performing his duty but not giving practical knowledge. The cultivators were also not familiar with the subject matter of the talks given by the experts. In most cases, the experts suggested "For further details contact block office". Such recommendations are beyond the reach of an average cultivator of Ismailpur. The cultivators complained about the language used in programme presentation having urban touch which, they felt, was difficult to follow.

In spite of the above-mentioned difficulties, some of the cultivators learnt about many innovations like mechanized agriculture and soil testing. Sometimes they also felt that these programmes were meant for rich cultivators only as they lacked the resources to meet the expenses suggested by television programmes. But they appreciated all those programmes in which no additional expenditure were suggested.

Television viewing also led to adoption of agriculture innovations. Three case studies of such adoptions are presented here.

Janak seed

On 20 and 21 October 1975 two ten minute documentaries on Janak, a high-yielding variety of wheat seed, were telecast. It was recommended for cultivators from Bihar. The programme of 21 October 1975 was repeated again on 28 October 1975. These progrommes were in lecture-demonstration format. In the demonstration, method of sowing in a straight line was emphasized. After a lapse of two weeks, in agricultural programmes of 11 November 1975 reference of Janak seed was made again. While discussing late sowing of wheat on 26 November and 2 December 1975 Janak was also recommended. Repeated recommendations led several discussions amoung the cultivators of Ismailpur.

In the first week of November 1975, the block officials were instructed by the State Government to provide fertilizer loan to those cultivators who would accept one bag (40 kg.) of Janak seed. It was to be distributed through the Multi-Purpose Cooperative Society. The price of this seed was fixed at Rs. 2.14 per kilogram which was much higher than the normal wheat price available in the market. The VLW approached the cultivators to promote the scheme. This led to distribution of loan and seed to seven cultivators of Ismailpur. By this time, Janak seed was repeatedly discussed on television and among the cultivators of the village. The availability of seed at their doorstep created an interest and sense of experimentation among them. Due to demonstration effect and under the influence of other cultivators, eight cultivators (seven of Awadhiya *jati* and one from Teli *jati*) having varying sizes of land holding (two to twenty acres) sowed Janak in smaller plots. Out of these eight cultivators, five were frequent viewers and two of them were occasional viewers. One of the cultivators though not a viewer was influenced by his son who was a viewer. Except two cultivators who were educated below secondary level, others were illiterates.

Further probing indicated that for seven cultivators the first source of information about the Janak seed was television alone. The eighth cultivators happend to be the younger brother of the Mukhia. It was thought that the first source of information for him might have been the Mukhia himself because of his close contact with the block development office. However, the Mukhia's brother emphatically denied this contention and mentioned that this first source of information was the television.

Other recommendations of Janak seed like irrigation could not be followed as strictly as it was told on television by the cultivators. On 13 December 1975, a special programme on irrigation was telecast when the cultivators of Ismailpur compared their irrigation method with that of the television recommendation. They realized that they could not follow the recommendation. This led to discussion among the cultivators and a proposal for late irrigation was mooted by them. It was hoped that if the television instructions were followed strictly, they would get better yield. However, due to other constraints no one except the Mukhia's brother could irrigate his field four times ; instead the others did it twice or thrice.

Harvesting results were not promising and the actual yield was relatively less when compared with IR-27 variety of seed that was sown a year before. Later on, it was found out that the Janak seed supplied was not properly tested for germination which might have been one of the reasons for low yield. Due to very high credibility of television messages, many of the cultivators thought that the low yield was due to inaccurate steps that were followed by them.

Disease of sugarcane

(a) One eleven minute documentary on pest control on sugarcane was telecast on 10 September 1975. This was related to the *Pyralis* pest. It was said that it effects the sugarcane and the green leaves turns yellow because of loss of chlorophyll and the infection generated by the white egg of the pest. It was suggested that affected yellow leaves should be plucked and burnt, and 10 per cent Barium-hydrochloride of Endrin or Paraffin should be sprayed to prevent the pest.

Among the adult viewers there were many cultivators. Shioshankar, a 20-year old young Awadhiya was one among them. He is a non-matric and his father owns only two acres of land. He seems to be happy-go-lucky always singing and making fun of others. He views the television whenever he gets time. He is friendly to most of the youth of Southern Ward though he lives at a distance of nearly 600 m. from the television centre.

On 10 September 1975, Shioshankar viewed the programme alongwith his friends and left for home without discussing with anybody. On the following day, while the researcher was returning from the village market, Shioshankar met him on the way. He was seriously thinking about the *Pyralis* pest as he was sure about its infestation in his field. He also told that he would spray Endrin to control the pest attack. He also stated that neither this pest nor the pesticide was ever known to him, and he had never used any insecticide or pesticide. He credited the television for giving information.

He could remember only Endrin out of the three pesticides recommended. He brought a small tin of liquid Endrin (about 250 ml.) and sprayed it in the field of 0.15 acre of sugarcane. He utilised an old bamboo pipe as sprayer, which he used during Holi festival, and sprayed the Endrin, mixing it in about 40 litres of water (two pitchers).

(b) Shyam, a regular television viewer, is a 21-year old non-matric Awadhiya having four acres of land in the household. He is one of the very "social" persons of this village and has contacts with many people from other villages. He goes to the nearby city atleast once in a month and also watches movies. He is progressive enough to adopt new ideas. His elder brother is a VLW and most of the informations regarding agriculture is received in this village through his VLW brother. Shyam's hobby is to organize things. When the television came in the village, he got associated with and assisted the custodian in the operation of the television and in audience control. He also helped the researcher in many ways during his fieldwork. He is a resident of Southern Ward near to the centre.

On 22 October 1975, a 13-minute documentary about the development of sugarcane industry was telecast. About 80 cultivators saw the programme. Shyam was one of them. In this programme, an expert illustrated field shots and the close up of some plants and their cross sections. The expert mentioned that if the inner side of stalk gets red in colour, the plant is supposed to be infected with *sukhada* disease and such plants should never be selected for seeding.

Next day, Shyam discussed the matter of *sukhada* disease with his father in front of Rajgir Singh of Awadhiya *jati* who happened to be there on a courtesy visit at that time. Shyam also showed one diseased plant and convinced them repeatedly with the example of television. His father agreed with him and decided to harvest the sugarcane. They also influenced the decision of another rich Awadhiya cultivator—Devendra Singh. He also decided to harvest sugarcane. Though his crop was not so infected, he had the fear that the infected plants would harm other plants. Devendra Singh was also a viewer but he missed viewing last night's programme.

By 29 October 1975, the sugarcane of Shyam and Devendra Singh were harvested and jaggery was prepared from it. On contacting Rajgir Singh, it was reported that he had discussed this matter with his son Shankar who told him that his field was not infected as he had already taken preventive measures by spraying Endrin in the initial attack of *pyralis*. This was done of course, on the advice of the experts on television.

Tub and lantern method

'The tub and lantern' method of killing insects infesting paddy was shown on television sometime in the month of November 1975. The programme illustrated the method. According to the suggestion, a ditch having central brick elevated platform should be dug. The ditch should be filled with water below the level of the brick platform. A lantern should be kept on the brick platform for the whole night. The insects would be attracted towards the light and die in the water.

This method was used by an illiterate old cultivator of Teli *jati* owning about five acres of land. Next day, when he found that the ditch was full of dead insects, he called others to see. The other villagers appreciated this method because it did not require anything more than what they had with them, and the cost was very little.

Animal husbandry

Out of 532 hardcore programmes, only 53 programmes were on animal husbandry. Table 9.3 shows the distribution of animal husbandry programmes by topic and format. The topics include artificial insemination, diseases of cattle, fishery, poultry, dairy, and sheep rearing. These programmes were in interview, talk, lecture and discussion (26.4%) ; demonstration (9.4%) documentary, film and story (58.5%) formats. A few programmes were also in graphics and still format.

The viewers liked the documentary, film and story formats. They did not like the interview, talk, lecture, and discussion formats, though it constituted one fourth of the programmes.

TABLE 9.3 : **Animal husbandry programmes by topic and format**

Topic	*Format*				*Total*
	Interview Talk Lecture Discussion	*Demonstration*	*Documentary film/ story*	*Graphic Stills*	
Artificial insemination			6.5		3.8
Better breeding	21.5		9.7		11.3
Disease of cattle	21.5			100.0	11.3
Fisheries	28.6	20.0			9.4
Poultry	7.1	80.0	16.1		18.9
Dairy	14.2		12.9		11.3
General care	7.1		35.5		22.6
Sheep rearing			19.3		11.3
Total	26.4	9.4	58.5	5.7	100.0 (53)

Viewers' preference and reactions

The viewers enjoyed the programmes on animal husbandry but the suggestions made with the use of technical terms for diseases and drugs were not followed by them. The suggestions of the experts to contact the Block Animal Husbandry Officer was criticized as "the so-called free" services were not available to the villagers. Programmes on poultry inspired a few Awadhiya and Teli *jati* viewers, but none except one adopted the poultry-keeping scheme due to fear of the disease *ranikhet* which kills all birds at one time. In such emergencies the services of the veterinarian would not be available.

Observed change

Poultry

The repetitive programmes on poultry and bird care initiated some discussions among the viewers. As mentioned in Chapter 3, all except the old Awadhiyas eat meat and poultry. A few youths planned to raise poultry. The problem was finance, and a place to keep the birds.

Finally, two persons were ready to invest money. S.N. Shah, a 40-year old teli having nearly ten acres of land decided to establish a broad in his mango orchard. Being the head of the household and a *jati* leader, it was possible for him to do so. But he could not do so till the termination of the fieldwork in 1976. The other man—Prem Singh, a 28-year old matriculate Awadhiya having nearly 12 acres of land made arrangements to keep poultry in the verandah of his house. Being a member of a large household, he faced serious opposition from his elder brothers. He was bold enough to resist them. He contacted the Block Animal Husbandry Officer who advised him to take some training in poultry farming. Without taking any such training, Singh started his poultry farm with 75 birds in the month of September, 1976.

Health, hygiene and nutrition

Table 9.1 shows that 11.4 per cent or 194 instructional programmes were devoted to health, hygiene and nutrition, covering different topics like disease, its cure, preventive measures, cleanliness and general health, *yoga* (physical exercise), and nutritious food and its preparation. Table 9.4 shows that almost, 50 per cent of these pro-

TABLE 9.4 : **Health, hygiene and nutrition programmes by topic and format**

Topic	*Format*					*Total*
	Interview Discus-sion Talk	*Demons-tration*	*Docum-entary Drama*	*Graphic Stills*	*Cartoon Film*	
Disease and its cure	34.4	14.7	17.6	41.6	42.9	27.3
Nutritious food and its preparation	17.5	16.4	23.5	16.7		15.5
Preventive measures	36.0		23.5	16.7		21.1
Cleanliness and general health	15.5	3.3	35.4	25.0	57.1	15.5
Yoga		65.6				20.6
Total	50.0	31.4	8.8	6.2	3.6	100.0 (194)

grammes were in the form of lecture, talk and discussion, whereas in 31.4 per cent programmes a demonstration format was used.

Responses to health programmes

Viewing of health programmes had considerable effect on the village life. A few Awadhiya women started thinking in terms of the vitamin content in vegetables. Boys, though they were tardy in following the instructions for cleanliness, quoted the advice given on television. A programme on round worms and the advice to wear shoes as a preventive measure was criticized by poor villagers but on the other hand it also inspired the women of a rich Teli household to purchase wooden footwear. The lecture and demonstration on the items of indigenous treatment attracted the attention of a few women.

Yogabhyas became popular among the youth of the village who viewed it, and practised some yoga postures in the wrestling ground. Before the introduction of television, they played *kabaddi* and practised wrestling. Some young men had been doing other physical exercises like *dand baithak* and *shirashasan* and when the programme of *Yogabhyas* was introduced, they switched over to practising yoga. Like other physical exercises, this also did not cost anything in terms of money or any investment. It was learnt that the demonstration of *yoga* was presented lucidly with clear instructions. The demonstrator sustained the attraction with his last sentence—"Next time more useful exercises will be shown". Another reason for its popularity had been told that "one feels energetic after *yoga*". The format of demonstration was well-liked both in the case of indigenous treatment and *Yogabhyas*. Lecture, talk, and discussion formats were less liked because the talk on general health and disease included technical words which the villagers did not follow. The viewers enjoyed cartoons.

Observed change

Acceptance and rejection of a health idea : The evening telecast of 23 October 1975, a ten-minute cartoon has on *ankush krimi* (hookworm). In this programe a healthy man walking around bare footed was shown. A hookworm got stuck in his leg and punctured the skin of the foot (sole) and went into the body. It had disturbed the total physiology of the body by sucking the blood and the man became weak. With this. the symptoms of the disease were told along with the details of precautions. The advice by the expert was to wear footwear and develop healthy habits. The announcer summarised the talk by giving emphasis on putting on shoes whenever going to the field or working in the mud. This programme was seen by about 300 persons of Ismailpur and viewers of nearby villages.

Killi Singh, a middle-aged Awadhiya having one acre of land was one among the viewers. His immediate reaction to the programme was not known. Next morning, he was discussing this issue with his neighbours. He rejected the idea of wearing shoes while working in the field, saying that it was all meant for rich persons. He said that though worms were harmful, to wear shoes all the time was not possible in the village situation as one had to work all the times in the mud. He posed a question with sarcasm "What do you do when the hands go inside the mud during transplantation of paddy?". Similar criticisms were offered by some other rich and poor, educated and illiterate viewers of different *jatis*.

Later Mishirlal Sah informed that his daughter had always appreciated the programme on hookworm and many a times put pressure upon him for purchasing chappals and finally got a pair of *khadaun* (wooden footwear).

Mishirlal Sah, a 40-year old Teli owning 6 acres of land, is himself educated upto the tenth standard. In his household, a lot of attention is paid towards education of females. The standard of living of his household is comparatively higher than others in the village. He has relatives in other towns also. His daughters are known to be 'fashionable girls' in the village. He is a 'progressive' cultivator having a diesel pumping set.

His daughter Manju, a 15-year old student of sixth standard was a casual viewer of television, but in the beginning, she used to come almost regularly. Manju saw the hookworm programme, it appealed to her and she brought the attention of her parents to it and also instigated her other sisters and relatives concerning the use of footwear. (It might be one reason that as she was a fashionable girl, she might have thought it a better way to convince her parent for purchasing chappals). Time and again, she extended her demand. Purchase of chappals in the family was viewed as a costly affair. But her father agreed to purchase wooden footwear. She bought it from a hawker of the village.

First of all, other women of the Ward laughed at Manju. But she continued motivating her aunt and friends. After one week, the wife and daughter of Wakeel Thakur (a barber) purchased wooden footwear. Neelam, the daughter of Wakeel Thakur was a friend of

Manju and this household also had a good income from outside and Neelam is educated upto the seventh class.

Seeing two more women wearing footwear the daughters of Shyamnandan Sah, Meena (14 years) and Prameela (11 years), became interested in buying the footwear. Initial motivation was provided by Manju. Two more pairs of wooden footwear were purchased. Now they all persuaded other women of the household to purchase footwear. The Wife of Jallandhar Prasad, after one month, purchased the same for her daughter and herself.

So, in total, till the termination of the field work, seven pairs of footwear were purchased. All these households were fairly educated (particularly in the case of females) and were well-to-do and also had sufficient outside contacts.

Idea of vitamin

The researcher used to cook his meal in the field. On January 18, 1976, before cooking vegetables he was peeling potatoes when 30-year old Mrs. Sumitra Singh, a regular television viewer stopped by to ask the time. She saw the researcher peeling potatoes. She immediately commented "What are you doing ? How many times has the television told us not to peel the skin because it contains vitamins. If we do not follow, we have an excuse as we are illiterates. But you are a well-educated person, why do you not practice as shown on television. Moreover, you view television daily". The researcher could not answer her.

The above incidents indicates how some ideas are getting accepted slowly.

Idea of cleanliness

Umesh is a 12-year old boy from Southern Ward. He is a student of sixth standard in the Fattehpur Middle School. He views television almost daily. Yogendra Singh, another 50-year old man of the same Ward is a teacher in another village. Though he lives in the same Ward, he watches television once or twice in a month.

It was early February 1976. There was very little water in the *chaur* and the canal was filled with still dirty water. Yogendra Singh was taking a bath in the canal when Umesh was passing through that way. He commented upon Shri Singh "You had seen television programmes many a times. Did not you hear the man on television saying that one should not take bath in still water". He told the researcher, who happened to be there, that he (the reseacher) should make Shri Singh understand that to take a bath in still and dirty water is not good.

Fomily planning

Of the total programmes 4.7 per cent or 81 programmes were devoted to family planning (*see* Table 9.1). These programmes covered the general problems and the motivational aspect, means and devices of family planning, and the value of sons and daughters. Table 9.5 provides a detailed breakdown of the programmes by content and format. The table shows that almost 90 per cent of the programmes were related to general problems and the motivational aspects of family planning. Almost 42 per cent of these programmes were documentaries. In the other 38.3 per cent programmes, drama, puppet shows, songs and dances were used for conveying the messages of family planning (*see* Table 9.5).

TABLE 9.5 : **Family planning programmes by topic and format**

	Format						
Topic	*Inter-view Discuss-ion Lecture*	*Lecture Inter-view Demons-tration*	*Docum-entary Film*	*Drama Puppet Song Dance*	*Graphic Stills*	*Car-toon Film*	*Total*
Means and Devices of Family Planning	10.0		2.9				2.5
General Problems and Motivation	30.0	100.0	97.0	93.5	100.0	100.0	87.6
Value of son and daughter	60.0			6.5			9.9
Total	12.3	1.2	42.0	38.3	3.7	2.5	100.0 (81)

Awareness and action

The underlying assumption of the family planning programmes was that it would persuade the viewers to take a positive decision regarding the adoption of family planning. Out of different formats, the documentary films were enjoyed by the viewers most. A few young males of different *jatis* comprehended the problem of more children. But their awareness did not ensure their adoption of family planning due to different socio-religious values associated with a son or daughter, and fear of failure and complications of the operation.

Out of nine persons of different *jatis* and economic status who had undergone vasectomy, only one person—Nagendra Thakur, a 28-year old illiterate Hajam owing one acre land, credited television programmes for providing motivation. After two sons he did not want any more children. Family planning workers were also trying to motivate him but it was the visual impact of the television programmes which helped in his decision. He was a regular viewer.

Four or five villagers (all of adult age group and Awadhiya *jati*) protested against the family planning camp, held in Ismailpur in the month of March 1976. They did not allow any one to attend the camp. The plea given by one 50-year-old matric-pass television viewer, a teacher of Awadhiya *jati* who was the main force behind the protest, was that when people and the government talk of television, we also want television type treatment from the doctors.

Analysing the above mentioned description it can be said that the programmes could not yield good results except to provide entertainment and knowledge to the viewers.

The above descriptions indicate that the repetitive exposure of instructional programmes on SITE objective areas generated some awareness among the viewers of Ismailpur. In some cases it also led to the adoption of innovations where extra cost was not involved or only some modifications in the existing practices was needed. The programmes on animal husbandry and health did not show results because they needed help of the development agents who are not freely and readily available to them. In the next chapter, the other instructional programmes and its effects will be analysed.

10

TELEVISION FOR INTEGRATION AND UPLIFTMENT

SOCIAL effects of television communication have been studied by a number of scientists. Apart from its intended and planned effects, there are some 'side' or 'unintended' effects. In Chinese communications study, Liu (1971) indicated that the mass media were necessary but not a sufficient cause of national integration because the whole impact depended, to a large extent, on the activities of the leadership who used the media. Evaluating the leadership's repeated chanting of Mao's thoughts over radio in China, Pool (1973) found the media were unable to prove much of its utility. But to Pool, this is not the failure of the technique (media), rather the content, context, receiver's perception and analysing capacity of the listeners were responsible for its failure. Lazarsfeld and Merton (1971) have different views on this issue. They think that the primary effects of the mass media is the maintenance of the status quo. According to them, media functions as just one element in a highly complex society and unless it is supplemented by face-to-face contacts, it can hardly be effective. McQuail (1977) feels that the mass media can attract and direct attention of problems and its solution.

In the Indian context, Lakshman Rao (1966) expects communication to help the public to know the government plans and programmes. During SITE, the softcore programmes were used to let the viewers know about the world and the people outside the village ; the developmental activities and the government plans, specially under the 20-point economic programme. Sachchidananda and Jha (1980) studied the impact of the 20-point economic programme and found that television helped the poor to know about it. Accordingly, they got some of the facilities, with the help, persuasion, and follow-up efforts of the members of the Communist Party of India in the village. Agrawal (1981) thought that the television can act as instigator and torchbearer for creating an egalitarian rural system.

Apart from other areas of the SITE objectives, the television attempted to improve social education to promote social harmony and a sense of social integration among the villagers. As indicated in Table 9.1, 253 or 14.8 per cent programmes covered such topics highlighting many cultural and social aspects of India. Table 10.1 shows that a major portion of these programmes (29.2%) were informative providing messages on social evils and individual responsibilities, alongwith preaching on moral issues (17.0%). Attempts were made to mobilise youth towards the social services. The programmes on National Service Scheme (NSS) and Youth Parliament aimed at achieving this. They were covered under the heading of informative programmes.

A major part of the instructional programmes covering areas other than the SITE objectives were on the 20-point economic programme (39.9%, *see* Table 10.1). Television was used to

TABLE 10.1 : **Instructional programmes other than SITE objectives by topic and format**

Topic	*Format*					*Total*
	Interview Discussion Lecture	*Film Documentary Indian News Review*	*Play Story*	*Song Drama*	*Graphic Still Cartoon*	
National integration	6.4	8.5	11.9	38.5	33.2	11.5
20-Point Economic Programme	48.9	41.0	31.3	61.5	11.1	39.9
Moral aspects	6.4	9.4	43.3	—	—	17.0
Informative programme	38.3	38.5	9.0	—	55.6	29.2
Adult education	—	2.6	4.5	—	—	2.4
Total	18.6	46.2	26.5	5.1	3.6	100.0 (253)

make the village aware about the 20-point economic programme (for details of the programmes, see Appendix A). From the start of SITE, the importance of this programme, priority, implementation, and its effects on the lives of the rural poor and the tribals were highlighted.

Little over 45.2 per cent of the programmes telecast were film documentaries, directl taken from the Indian News Review, followed by 26.5 per cent plays and stories which were quite popular. A little less than 20 per cent programmes used lecture and discussion format which were not popular.

The analysis in this chapter is divided into two sections. The first section analyses the effects of general programmes on the national integration on the village youth and other viewers. In the second section, the effects of the 20-point economic programme have been presented.

In the programmes for integration and social education, short films on India's geography, natural resources, economic development, the green revolution, industries, educational expansion and scientific researches and such gave information about India's progress. Social evils like the dowry system inspired some films, so too did alcoholism. A film entitled "Gold in one fields" attempted to glorify rural life as against the attraction of migrating to cities. Smuggling and blackmarketing were decried and the 20-point programme's promises to come down heavily on such activities were reinforced.

The programme *Ek Desh Anek Pradesh* (one Country many States) was appreciated by most of the viewers including women. The viewers pleaded "We are not furtunate to go and see these places but television has shown us from distance". Some of them could tell the name of the state to which the character belonged by merely seeing the dress pattern, folk song and dances.

The literate youth liked the programmes on Youth Parliament, National Service Scheme, invention series, and Indian News Review. According to them, it widened their knowledge and generated a sense of responsibility for doing something for the village. Young girls (both literate and illiterate), realized the need for education and a few of the illiterate Awadhiya girls showed an inclination to continue to learn, read and write after viewing. The documentaries demonstrating the activities and plays, highlighting the social values were preferred most. Talevision viewing also led to the rise of the Yuva Dal (Youth Force). A case study of the Yuva Dal is presented.

Yuva Dal

The programmes on Youth Parliament, the National Service Scheme and other social welfare activities had stimulated a few youths of Ismailpur to do some community service. They formed a group which was joined by most of the high school students of Ismailpur and the jobless youth. The name of this group was given as Yuva Dal. They started their activities with the cleaning of the Dhunia Ward, which was quite dirty. When the youth of Awadhiya *jati* started sweeping the frontage of their houses, it made a good impression upon the villagers and they started sweeping themselves.

The group became active and the members were seen discussing their next programme. Villagers, particularly the Dhunia were satisfied over this development as instead of harassing people, the youth were engaged in planning some 'good' things. The leader of the Yuva Dal declared that any complaint against anyone could be intimated to the Dal and they would go through the matter and take necessary action.

In the month of December 1975, one notorious youth of Awadhiya *jati*, who also happened to be a member of the Yuva Dal, committed a crime of stealling one cock from a poor Dhunia household. The matter was brought to the notice of the Dal and in its meeting the members decided a cash punishment of rupees ten and caning in public. This was an action which no one else could have taken against this young man. But the group collected ten rupees and gave it to the Dhunia household as a compensation for the cock and the culprit was caned ten times in front of villagers. This act gave very high credit to the group. On the eve of January 1976—first day of the year—they organized a contributory community feast (*banbhoj*) which was attended by about 80 persons from almost all the *jatis* of the village. The Dusadh (Scheduled Caste) helped in cooking and the Dhunia served the meal. It was praised by many villagers.

In the month of April 1976, a team of workers belonging to Nehru Yuvak Kendra, Muzaffarpur stopped over at Ismailpur, the Local Dal helped this group in organizing meetings and joined hands in *sramadan* (physical labour). The coordinator of the Nehru Yuvak Kendra expressed the desire to patronise this local group and assured full cooperation if the group was organized for social upliftment.

The Yuva Dal became a threat to the power group in the village in many matters. The Yuva Dal decided to revive the functioning of the library. They demanded the accounts of the old books from a rich villager who very much liked the idea of reopening it, but he was not interested in giving the accounts of the old books. Finally, he manipulated the whole affair. A few respected villagers persuaded the Dal not to demand the account of the books. Instead they suggested to start afresh which was a difficult task as a lot of money was needed to buy the books.

There were three complaints against the Mukhia. One regarding illegal occupancy of someone's land. Two, about the Mukhia instigating a villager not to allow his neighbour to construct a house next to him. And the third was about the Mukhia's own servant who was beaten severely for non-payment of a loan. When the Mukhia was approached, it was said that he did not entertain the Dal members and told them to mind their business. Dal raised their voice jointly and tried to mobilize the village opinion against the Mukhia. The Mukhia supposedly implicated two active members of the Dal in a court case and threatened others of similar consequences. A similar hint was allegedly given by the sub-inspector of police, Goraul, to the members of the Dal. Many members got intimidated due to police interference.

A few youth were pressurized by their parents not to go against the Mukhia. But they took courage from the exhortations on television that "the citizens should object to every wrong act, no matter who the culprit is". "Television says to save people from exploitation" or "Did you not see how the small kids were fighting against the hoarder, why not we ?" Atleast three times, the Dal members approached the researcher to write to the Collector against the Mukhia. When the researcher declined to write the complaint, they became angry and asked "Then why does the television ask us to inform the nearest government official ?"

Though the Dal was helpless in some of the cases, it gained popularity in the village and many villagers started relying on Dal. The block functionaries also started recognising Dal and began consulting it.

TELEVISION FOR UPLIFTMENT

The use of television for the promotion of the 20-point economic programme—commitment to the upliftment of the rural poor—

will be analysed in this section. Before analysing the data on this topic, a sample of programmes that were telecast is presented, followed by a short description of one of the poor households of Ismailpur who were the target audience of these programmes.

Impact of economic programme on cultivators

To illustrate the impact of the 20-point programme, interviews were conducted with cultivators. This conveyed the public opinion that since the Emergency, prices full and blackmarketing of inputs was reduced. Agricultural officials commended the Prime Minister for opening new avenues for the advancement of agriculture. A cultivator in Bharatpur who was interviewed claimed that television which he sees as part of the Emergency, gave him a lot of new information on agriculture. Others claimed that land was distributed and irrigation facility provided on an unprecedented scale. Animal husbandry was proclaimed to have received a big boost. The villagers were informed that extension workers were working extensively to bring news of new possibilities and benefits to cultivators. The compare then summarised the gains of tke Emergency for cultivators, and held out the promise of a bright happy future for all cultivators.

Impact on supply of agricultural equipment

Agricultural equipment is essential for profitable agriculture. Such equipment was to be made available to even the small cultivators due to special provisions made in the Prime Minister's new economic programme. A playlet reinforced this in the following manner :

> A poor cultivator and his wife are shown worrying about the need to educate their son for which they must improve the productivity of their land. He reads a newspaper by chance, and comes across descriptions of the twenty points : essential commodities are to be provided at controlled prices in student residence halls, books and stationery are to be made available at similar rates too, loans are available for agricultural purposes. Their worries are over.

Gains of emergency in Bihar

Special Secretary to the Bihar Cabinet gave a television talk on how zamindari abolition was not enough, and that the Prime Minister's new 20-point economic policy went a step further to free bonded labour. The accomplishment of the Bihar government were cited as follows : Electricity widely extended and house sites provided to the poor and so on. The Information Minister of Bihar gave a talk on implementation of the new economic programme in terms of providing avenues for self-employment, extension of education and health facilities, and the liberation of bonded labour.

Agriculture loans

Every man needs help in some form or another. The Prime Minister's 20-point programme was to meet the cultivator's needs for cash and kind, and relieve him from the clutches of the moneylender. The head of a village agriculture cooperative credit society in Jaipur district held a group discussion in his village which was televised. Previously, the moneylender charged exorbitant rates of interest and finally acquired the debtor's house, land and ornaments. The cultivator was born indebted, grew in debt, and died in debt. Now cultivators growing one crop without irrigation can get Rs. 1,500 in cash plus Rs. 1,500 worth of inputs.

All these benefits were to be available through cooperative societies. Membership in such societies was open, and shares could be bought according to individual capacity. The 20-point programme activated the functioning of cooperatives in the interest of progress of the common man.

PROFILE OF A RECIPIENT—A POOR HOUSEHOLD

Amidst the hutments of Dhunia Ward lives Saleem, a 21-year old man of Dhunia *jati*. Saleem grew up in the middle of these huts belonging to his fellow *jati* members. He has seen the *pucca* houses belonging to the rich Awadhiya villagers for whom he has been serving for the last ten years.

His mother recounted the past and said that some 30 years ago when she came to this village there was not even a single *pucca* house. This family was poor but the condition was not so miserable. Her husband was in the service of rich cultivator who provided just enough to live. Her husband had a small piece of land (about 0.03 acre) in which he used to grow vegetables and maize. Soon after her marriage, she also started working as agricultural labourer alongwith her younger brother-in-law and the other women of the ward. This way all the three members of the household were earning. After three years of marriage she gave birth to her first child—Raheem. The child was always sick. Her son's sickness had put her into trouble. Due to his sickness she could not work, and the income was less. She arranged the marriage of her brother-in-law and the family saving was spent on this occasion. She gave her ornaments to the new bride. Then Saleem was born.

Her brother-in-law separated and the land got divided. The increasing cost of living and almost static labour wage made life. hard. The landowners were not ready to increase the wage accordingly. Labourers like her did not have any alternative except to depend upon what the cultivators agreed to pay.

In these circumstances she did not even think of giving education to her sons. Her husband suffered some unknown disease. He developed severe back pain. She consulted diviners and village quacks. His health did not improve. She wanted to show him to the doctor but there was no money. The land and the hut was mortgaged but the money was not sufficient to meet the prolonged treatment. There was a heavy cut in the income and the cost on the treatment and diet of the patient was high. The only remaining ornament—a silver chain was sold. Raheem started working with a cultivator on a monthly salary of rupees fifteen only. All these efforts could not save Saleem's father.

During the course of treatment, she took a loan from the Mukhia. Her husband's death put her in further debt to the same moneylender—the Mukhia. For two years she confined with all the difficulties. But it became difficult to get even two meals. The income was not regular and the unexpected expenditure was there. For marriage or death of any relative, and any festival the only alternative was to take loan from the local rich villagers on 'high' interest, sometimes up to 25 per cent a month.

There was no way to repay the loan and at an early age of twelve, in the year 1966, Saleem joined the Mukhia household as a permanent servant on a monthly salary of rupees twenty only, in addition to two meals and a pair of cloth as yearly. The montly salary did not come to the household in full as half of it was adjusted against the interest of the loan his mother took from the Mukhia from time-to-time.

Saleem very much wanted to come out of the Mukhia's clutches because, according to him, he could earn more elsewhere. The

Mukhia had increased the salary from rupees twenty to thirty since 1974. But the problem was to get rid of the loan and they did not have any other property to dispose off. Raheem was married and he started his own cooking in the same house.

Saleem was not the only person facing this problem. Most of the labourers from Dhunia and Nonia *jatis* complained that it had became almost impossible to meet the daily expenditure in the low wages given to them. They wanted to leave the village and go to Patna or Calcutta where then could get more wages and regular jobs. Some of them have already gone to Patna to pull *rickshaw*. But the uncertainity of jobs in those places and the initial expenditure involved are handicaps. Getting financial assistance from any other source is out of question.

The small cultivators meet with almost similar fate. They depend solely upon their fertile land and what they get out of it is hardly sufficient to maintain the household, to educate their children, and to invest as input for the next crop. The marriage, death or any other function in the household, any accident or major sickness or the natural calamities like drought or flood, affect their budget. For some of them, the day-to-day expenditure puts them into debt. In these crisis situations they do not find any other alternative except to mortgage or sell their small pieces of land thereby inviting more crises in the future.

The responses

Television minimized the value of communication leader

As described in earlier chapters, in Ismailpur, mass media and urban contact is very poor. Very few persons travel to nearby towns. Villagers in general, do not have links with the block office. The Mukhia is the only person who has contacts with block officials and political leaders. Hence, he gets official communication and utilises it, if beneficial, for himself and interpretes it according to his perception.

The regular exposure related to the 20-point economic programme came to the villagers through television. Villagers could not comprehend the programme fully but they could understand the points related to the common problems of the village. These related to increase in labour wages and modification of *rehan-bharana* (mortgage land) rules according to which a man was to get his land back after seven years of mortgage. The poor who took money by mortgaging the land on *bharna* became hopeful of getting their land back. The Mukhia had taken land on *bharna* from Bigani Maosmat ten years ago. Bigani did not have any son, so her eldest son-in-law Suresh Singh, settled in the village, inherited the landed property. During the last four years, Suresh Singh tried hard to pay the loan with interest and to get the 1½ acres of land back from Mukhia. But Mukhia did not agree to return the land. The total loan taken was only Rs. 300.

Suresh Singh, 35-years old matriculate Awadhiya was a television viewer. He was happy to learn about the new law. On 15 November 1975, Suresh Singh invited some of his relatives who were also related to the Mukhia to settle the land matter in a *jati* panchayat. The discussion went on for hours. After the discussion, Jagadeo Sah, another villager of Ismailpur, opined that the Mukhia was wrong on this issue because according to the television, after seven years one would be entitled to restore the land without paying even a single paisa. This rule he knew only through the television. This version of Jagadeo Sah was objected to by Lala Singh, another villager of Ismailpur who said that this rule was not applicable to the person having more than one acre of land. He asserted this by saying that Mukhia was the person who could not be wrong. But Jagadeo Sah and Shyamnandan Singh were not ready to listen to him. According to them, when it was conveyed by television that this rule was applicable to all, how could Suresh Singh and the Mukhia be above it. In their opinion, the Mukhia could be wrong but not the television. The above analysis supports the view that the information of the Mukhia, who was supposed to be the most reliable source of information in official matters, could no longer challenge an average villager due to the help of the message conveyed by television.

Analysis of phases

The 20-point economic programme was announced on July 1975, but it had been introduced to the villagers through television almost with the start of SITE. Every day there were some messages relating to the 20-point economic programme. The villagers did not know the details of it. They could comprehend only those points which were connected with their village situation. These were about the abolition of bonded labour system, abolition of *Rehan* and *Bharana* system, increase in labour wages, fair dealing to the villagers through various welfare and developmental activities and fall in prices. Altogether 5.9 per cent of the total programmes were shown on the 20-point programme (*see* Table 10.1).

The response to the 20-point programmes by the villagers of Ismailpur could be analysed in four phases :

(i) Phase of curiosity; (ii) Phase of expectation;
(iii) Phase of conflict; and (iv) Phase of indifference

The first phase of the programme attracted viewers and others towards it and the people were trying to know more about it. Everybody was curious, except the anti-congress faction who considered it as propaganda and an election stunt. They got some knowledge of the 20-point economic programme and the work being done under this banner. It continued till September 1975.

The second phase started from October and the labourers developed some hopes that their wages would be increased, village youths thought of reform in the system that some employment opportunities would be made available in the village, they would get support from Bank, there would be fair dealing in the village and they would also be given opportunities to develop the village as well as themselves. They started thinking of re-opening the library. Villagers in general had high expectations of better developmental as well as welfare services from administration. But the rich cultivators had a sense of fear that they would be caught by the administration for their maltreatment and exploitation of labourers. Thus they expected some hard times in the coming future.

The third phase after December 1975 was witnessed with tension all around. Labourers demanded high wages as per government rates of Rs. 5 a day instead of the existing rate of rupees two to rupees three per day. The landholders flatly refused to give a higher rate and said "These not for villages, if you want, you ask the television to give you high wages as well as work". Landless labourers asked "When will these welfare schemes come in operation in this village?". An answer given to the wife (by a husband) was "They are serving the city people first and if any thing will be surplus, will be given to us". Rich people made the television programmes responsible for instigating the labourers against landowners and they tried to disturb the functioning of television. The existing power in the village abused television because the youth became active in society and the poor were helped by them. The loans of the money lenders were forzen and they were applying physical force to recover it, of course, with a sense of fear. Moneylenders refused to give any further loan against the 20-point programme while bank facilities remained far from their reach. The government agencies had an extra burden which they had to accept willingly or unwillingly. This stage continued till May 1976.

In the last phase that is June 1976 onwards, people developed a sense of distrust for television because they could not see any activity in the village. Labourers could not find any other alternative except to depend upon the mercy of the large cultivators. The youth found themselves helpless because the exploiters had a strong footing and they received support from the local administration. The exploiters found themselves carefree from any outside interference and the developmental agencies took it as a part of their routine to which they need not give any special attention. Villagers became indifferent towards the message as well as the channel. The television lost, to some extent, it's credibility.

11

AFTER SITE

SO FAR, the analysis centred around the effects of television viewing on school children and the adults of Ismailpur. In this chapter the effect of SITE when it was withdrawn after July 1976 will be analysed in a longitudinal perspective. In order to do so, the village was revisited twice in the months of June-July 1977 and May 1980. In the subsequent fieldwork, attempts were made to follow the fate of those innovations which were adopted as a result of television viewing earlier along with other changes that might have occurred in the village.

The information about completion of SITE started appearing on television several weeks prior to 31, July 1976. One of the immediate effects of these announcements was increased viewer attendance. However, there were very few who believed that there would be no television programme after 31, July 1976. The last day programme was just to say good bye to SITE viewers and the literate viewers realized that it was really the end of SITE.

On 1 August 1976 six adult and nearly 15 children gathered near the television centre around 6.00 p.m. In another half an hour, the number increased and went up to 18 adults and nearly 25 children. They came to the researcher to ask whether the television had really stopped. Such gatherings continued for several days, but nothing appeared on television. In the beginning, they thought that it would start working after a few days once more, as it happened during April 1976 when the transformer had gone out of order.

For the majority of the villagers, the withdrawal of television left a void in their life. There used to be gathering of people every evening near the television centre even when it did not function in the past. But now nobody was there. The withdrawal had various kinds of reactions among the different categories of viewers. The vocal group were women, men, children and youth. Their reactions are analysed separately.

Women

The women, in general, felt that the television was a good means of recreation. They felt sad when the evening viewing stopped. It became a problem to pass their evening time. In the first few weeks, it seemed that the whole village remained inactive. As many of them had not seen movie, they had been happy that atleast they were able to see television. The young women faced to problems : (a) What to do in the evening? To talk to other women they had to go out of their homes which was, in many cases, objected to by the guardians. They feared that in gossiping, they would develop bitterness in their relations, and (b) If they remained at home they would be given work to do and now there was no excuse. On the other hand, the older women felt good because during SITE, their daughters-in-law and daughters went to see television leaving them alone at home and they had to look after all the home affairs. Now they remained at home and they fell free of home burden.

Women from Dhunia Ward and Hazamtoli reported that the clashes between women had increased due to the withdrawal. The reason behind it was that women who were interested in watching television used to prepare the night meal earlier, so they did not get enough time to sit in the lane and talk to other women, which minimized the clashes. But now the routine had changed. There was no need to cook early, hence gossiping with other women and occasionally picking quarrels was common.

Men

For adult viewers in an isolated village like Ismailpur, SITE meant more then entertainment and information. The evenings in the company of television started becoming a part of their daily life. Prior to the arrival of television the evenings were spent either in gossip groups or in bed or once in a while in ceremonies fairs, and festivels. But these occasional interludes had became a regular affair especially if there was power supply in the village. For the daily wage labourers the free entertainment and a place to spend the evening was gone after the completion of SITE. The immediate problem for them was to rearrange the evening schedule.

The teachers had mixed feelings. Though they felt unhappy about the withdrawal of television they were positive that now many students would start doing their homework regularly. Very soon the television-user teacher became irregular and the custodian disappeared from the village. The flour mill owner was happy that nobody put pressure on him for putting off the mill during viewing hours. The Mukhia was happy in whose opinion television viewing was responsible for instigating landless labourers against the rich. In the third week of August 1976 he stored fertilizer in the television room alongwith the set.

Children and the youth

The children and the youth of the village were the worst sufferers from the withdrawal. For them, the television centre had become a focal point of meeting, interacting, and exchanging news every evening. Due to the withdrawal of television the children and the youth lost an opportunity of viewing programmes and meeting each other. Both expressed their anguish in terms of "blank" evenings and forced studies, thrust on them by the elders. The youth, once again, felt devoid of information from external world. Again jobless youth started loitering in the lanes of the village a headache for the elders.

The labourers of Dhunia Ward, and Binkharia felt bad because after the whole day's tiring work they used to get free "entertainment". Now they sat idle. The masters of permanent servants do not allow them to sit without work but during SITE, they were themselves busy with the television and so the servants were relieved. After SITE, the cooking schedule reverted back to the before-SITE timings after about a fortnight. In a few Awadhiya households, it did not change till the termination of field work. Now women prepared the meals early, fed everyone early and went to sleep. Some of the evening gossip groups started reappearing after a month of SITE.

After SITE, the Muzaffarpur Doordarshan Kendra (DDK) was set up in 1978 to provide television services to Ismailpur and other villages of this area through terrestrial system. Now, television sets have been installed in two nearby villages Baksama and Premraj. But Ismailpur does not have a television, as explained by the officials, due to the difficult approach road of the village. Presently on an average, two hour daily power supply is available in Ismailpur and in the whole area, that too after 10 p.m. It was observed that power supply remained suspended continuously for as much as six-seven days at a time. Due to this reason, the viewing is so irregular that the custodians (according to the school teachers of Baksama and

Premraj) have stoped operating the set. Whenever the power supply is available, during transmission hours, the enthusiastic youth request the resident headmaster and science teacher of these schools to put on the television. Due to such an erratic power supply, almost none of the Ismailpur villagers have been able to view television after SITE.

The television is very much wanted by the villagers of Ismailpur. After its withdrawal from the village they have lost an important source of entertainment as well as information. During SITE, the television centre had become a meeting point for social interaction and communication as there was no other place where people from all *jatis* of the village could get together. According to the villagers, including the Mukhia's household, the television used to provide regular information. To them "If they have information today they would be in a position to use it tomorrow. But what could they do without it". They believe that once a person has learned something new from the television, he/she cannot forget it. Another thing which has bothered villagers of Ismailpur is that now television sets have been installed in Premraj and Baksama but not in Ismailpur. They feel left out and neglected.

THE VILLAGE AFTER FIVE YEARS

There seemed to be a little change in the villagers' conception of the village boundary between 1976 and 1980. Even today, as described in Chapter 3, the Northern Ward has not been very closely integrated with the rest of the village. Two reasons were given : the proximity of the settlement and minor clashes mainly for want of irrigation facilities. Their earliest animosity which started during SITE on the power supply issue though has stopped now, the old bitterness continues between Northern Ward and the rest of Ismailpur. The villagers consider this ward as a part of Fatehpur village. In 1975-76 fieldwork, very little interaction between villagers, block development office and other development agents were observed which seems to continue. The village level worker (VLW) who is expected to stay in the village does not stay. The village panchayat continues to be the pride possession of the Mukhia who uses its properties as his own. The Multi-purpose Cooperative Society closed down after 1978. It is because the earlier loans have not been returned and was badly manipulated by the Secretary of the Society. Postal services continue to be unsatisfactory. Even today, money orders are supposedly not delivered without a commission and letters are distributed in the tri-weekly market (*see* Chapter 4).

The only observable change is an appearance of a new motorcycle in the village purchased by the Post Master, and also a transistor radio given as a gift to a villager by his in-laws.

Janak seed

This high-yielding variety of wheat has become popular among the rich cultivators who could afford to irrigate their fields three to four times in the last five years. During the SITE, when the Janak seed failed to yield good results, the cultivators contributed its failure to the bad quality of seed. In the following years, the block agriculture unit provided plenty of Janak seed as agricultural loan. Janak seed also became available in the open market. Several medium and large cultivators adopted Janak seed and got good yield.

Kufri Sinduri Potato

During the SITE year, the television programmes repeatedly advised people to sow Kufri Sinduri variety of potato. Inspired by the television, Jamadar Singh wanted to sow it then. But it was a little late for sowing and the seed was not available. In the following season (1976-77), however, he arranged to get the seed from Muzaffarpur and experimented in a little piece of land. He could not follow all practices except to spray the ashes over the leaves which is a general practice for preventing the vegetable crops from pests. The yield was better than what he was getting from the earlier variety—*Kachchu*. The same seed was preserved for the next year and this led others to adopt Kufri Sinduri (and now the villagers grow only Kufri Sinduri). Singh, a 45-year old Awadhiya *jati* cultivator owning three acres of land, says that he did not hear anything about Kufri Sinduri except from the "krishi darshan" programme on television. He discussed the idea with his son and both of them decided to adopt it. Singh is an introverted person and he did not discuss about the new variety of potato seed with any body else. His son told others when it was a success.

Poultry

When Prem Singh started poultry farming, there was a lot of resentment in the Awadhiya *jati*, but he was quite bold. Singh and his friends quoted the television advice for adopting poultry. Singh learnt all about the care of the birds only through the television. After Singh's death, in 1977 his brothers did not like poultry keeping, hence, they sold the birds to Shyamnandan Shah who started his poultry in his orchard. After a few months, all the birds died due to the disease—Ranikhet (*tunki*)—as Shyamnandan Shah did not take proper care. In the late 1978, Shyamnandan Singh and the nephew of late Prem Singh brought two birds each against the will of the guardians. Later Ramamilan Singh also brought four birds. It is notable that all of them belong to Awadhiya *jati* and now poultry farming has almost been accepted in the Awadhiya *jati*.

Tub and lantern method

Asharfi Shah, who adopted tub and lantern method of killing insects during SITE (as described in Chapter 9) discontinued the practice. After SITE, in the winter of 1976, two Awadhiyas and one Teli youth experimented with this method of insect killing. They continued this experiment for three to four days and every time they found an almost similar influx of insects. They discontinued the practice because others were not doing the same and insects would be attracted from other plots to the plot in which the method is followed. This method was found very useful, particularly for a small plot of paddy field. It should be adopted by all the cultivators.

Some of the regular viewers who had shown an interest in television and adopted a few innovations had left the village. Shankar and Bhola Singh joined the army in 1978. Lala Singh went to Sisma Bajar to handle the tobacco business. Shyamnandan got involved in social and political affairs so that he hardly takes any interest in agriculture. But he claims to remember the instructions given for cartain agricultural practices.

Yuva Dal

As described in Chapter 10, the Yuva Dal (youth force) was formed and if got some importance in due course. Even after the death of its leader Prem Singh in 1977, the Yuva Dal continues to be a cohesive group. On every occasion they unitedly decide the course of action. The villagers think that the youth has developed a lot since the formation of Yuva Dal and its direction is right. Yuva Dal does not allow anybody to harm the poor. They have started taking interest in the village politics which has given them a sense of purpose and direction. Further, in no way do they harm any one.

The Mukhia and his henchmen, however, think that the Yuva Dal will harm the village. In their opinion, the Dal is not always supporting the right cause. Dal members are in competition with the Mukhia and try to pull him down as and when necessary. The Mukhia feels that this group is taking the shape of 'dacoit gang' and today or tomorrow its members would be behind the bars. It is because the Yuva Dal decided to oppose the Mukhia and supported an independent candidate from Khokhara village during the 1978 panchayat election. It is told that there was a lot of administrative interference and the Mukhia won the election using unfair means. Immediately after the election the Mukhia allegedly managed to implicate his opponent and three Yuva Dal members in a murder case. The Dal was in very bad shape then. The Dal members contacted the Lok Dal higher-ups for help whose party was in state power. They were saved from the murder charges. It costed a heavy amount of money and the Yuva Dal came close to the Lok Dal.

During the 1980 Assembly elections of Bihar the Mukhia contested the election on Congress (I) ticket from the nearby constituency—Vaishali. The members of Yuva Dal tried hard to mobile the opinion of the voters against the Mukhia. The Mukhia lost the election with a large margin. Apart from other factors, the Yuva Dal is held responsible for his defeat.

12

SUMMARY, CONCLUSION AND IMPLICATION

AMONG modern means of communication, television is considered as one of the most effective tools for education and development. In India, the cinema is confined in the urban areas and the field publicity units hardly reach village lanes. Television appeared late on the scene. Till the mid-Seventies, it remained an urban phenomenon due to technological limitations. This technological limitation was overcome by the gift of an advance technology—communication satellite. This led to the one year Satellite Instructional Television Experiment (SITE) ; from 1 August 1975 to 31 July 1976 in six states of India. SITE was conducted in 393 villages of North Bihar.

This study was undertaken to analyse the process of existing rural communication, the barriers of communication hindering rural development, and to study socio-cultural implications of satellite television. So far, major emphasis has been laid on studying the impact of television. In this work, an attempt has been made to understand the role and relevance of television in rural development.

The selection of a representative village was based on criteria like population size, *jati* composition and its distance from the urban centre to minimize urban influence. Actual field visits of a number of villages prior to fieldwork helped in the village selection. An eighteen months fieldwork was conducted in the village of Ismailpur. It enabled the researcher to come close to the villagers and extract relatively more authentic data. The total fieldwork was divided into three phases : (1) pre-SITE, (2) during-SITE, and (3) post-SITE. In the post-SITE period, the village was revisited twice ; in the year 1977 and 1978, for six weeks each time.

Ismailpur is located in Vaishali district of old Muzaffarpur, North Bihar. It is 37 km south of Muzaffarpur town. The villagers speak

Bajjika dialect of the Hindi language. The village settlement is scattered on either side of the road that passes through elevated land of the village. The 172 household having 1,016 souls live in six Wards or *tola*. They are divided into two religious groups and eight *jati* and *jati*—like groups. Numerically, economically and otherwise the village is dominated by a single *jati*—Awadhiya. The land distribution is such that only two households have more than 20 acres of land whereas nearly 30 per cent are landless among whom a majority are agricultural labourers. The agro-based economy of the village depends mainly upon maize, and tobacco as cash crop.

Educationally, the village is backward. The mass media exposure is limited to listening of film songs through radio, that too by very few. Medical facilities are not adequate and the villagers rely more on the village quacks than on the doctors and their costly allopathic medicine. The village has electricity, a health sub-centre, a lower primary school, and a multi-purpose cooperative society. These institutions hardly meet the developmental needs of the village.

The village has its own verbal communication system which is face-to-face and expressed through oral gestures and symbols and are codified and decodified by the villagers. The learning of communication starts with the process of socialization. Being interpersonal and direct, it involves various levels of communication viz., household, *jati*, village, and occupation. In the analysis, sex-linked normative behaviours have been identified which are manifested in role relationships, dress pattern, and nature of work.

The contribution of mass media, that is radio, newspaper, and cinema for rural development is almost non-existent. Official channels involved in developmental activities, operating through village level worker and other workers are functioning unsatisfactorily. These officials are not regular in their task ; moreover, they approach the rich and large cultivators first. The rich and large cultivators block most of the information. They reach the poor and landless labourers only if it is allowed to pass by them.

The Sonepur fair contributes quite a bit in providing developmental information on agriculture, health, and family planning. Sonepur information gets further through the visitors who discuss it in the gossip groups. For the first time, on 1 August 1975, the villagers of Ismailpur saw moving pictures with sound on a 21-inch television screen in a community viewing situation. In the begining, the television attracted people from neighbouring villages also. After the novelty effect was over, the average attendance in the evening was around 80 persons of both sexes of which children were nearly 25 per cent. The seasonal variations and agricultural cycle were two factors that effected the audience size. The males of 15 to 24 years of age and the females of 4 to 14 years of age were numerically more than the others among the audience. More than half of the audience were illiterate, largest among them being housewives. Among the literate viewers, one-fourth had received secondary education. The average viewer size of students did not exceed more than 35 in the morning transmission.

There seems to be a somewhat uniform acceptance of television among the villagers of Ismailpur. Except that men and women sat separately while viewing television no other discriminations were observed. The custodian as well as the user-teacher performed their duties irregularly and inefficiently. The reasons were the faulty selection of uninterested persons and unattractive incentives given to them. The language of the programmes, though Hindi had an urban touch which created difficulty in comprehension. The viewers preferred programmes in the local dialects. The functioning of the set was quite satisfactory, except for the erratic electricity supply.

The 22½ minutes morning transmission meant for school children could not yield much except that students of the school learnt to make paper dolls and pickedup a few new Hindi words. The reasons for low comprehension are many :

(i) the students were of lower grades whereas the programmes were meant for students of higher grades ;
(ii) the standard of teaching through television was higher than the standard of the village school ;
(iii) in village school, there were no facilities to explain the things to the students that were shown on television ;
(iv) the user-teacher did not play any role in explaining the programme ; and
(v) the distance between the television centre and the school was fairly high, which kept the students running between the two points and getting exhausted in the process.

The 'training through television' for school teachers shows that the same can fruitfully be used for training. But. careful selection should be made of motivated teachers and a proper coordination and monitoring system should be evolved for its appropriate utilization.

Nearly 150 hours of television exposure in various instructional areas in different formats aroused mixed reactions. The vieweres reacted and responded to these programmes in accordance with the specific topics and formats, relevent to their needs.

The most preferred formats were field demonstration, documentary, and play in order of preference. The lecture and discussion formats were least liked by the viewers.

Television viewing led to discussions among the viewers and they talked on vitamins and health among follow-viewers. The ideas of "new" health practices like wearing shoes to protect the body against hookworm had mixed reactions—part acceptance and part rejection. The animal husbandry programmes could arouse some discussion and adoption. After initial protest against poultry farming by the fellow-*jati* members, an Awadhiya youth was able to adopt it. There were few apparent signs of adoption in the field of agriculture. The cultivators of Ismailpur adopted the suggested innovations, mostly requiring little or no external help and additional expenditure. Other recommendations did not stand and chance of adoption because most of them involved some input which the cultivators did not have and some expert help which they could not get.

The programmes related to the topics other than the SITE objectives inspired the village youth to take up social activity. They united together to help the poor and fought against exploitation. But such an action threatened the existing power structure of the village which was exploitative in nature. When these two forces confronted, the police and the local administration came forward to support the exploiters. Those who came forward were completely at loss as the television did not prepare them for such a situation.

The 20-point economic programme—a top priority programme for rural upliftment—could attract a large number of viewers as it had some attractive programmes which might have helped them. It created false hope among those who were helpless. They demanded their rights for the benefits offerred only through the television. But the wide gap between what they expected due to the television information and what they actually experiences to serious tensions all around. These programmes were viewed as burdens by those in responsible positions. It led to indifference towards the message as well as the television among poor. The rich were glad that they still held away. In spite of all these, the television had higher credibility than other sources of information. Statements like "Television does not give wrong information" and "Television does not lie" are indicative of its credibility.

CONCLUSIONS AND IMPLICATIONS

The study clearly reflects a positive role that a medium like television can play in rural development, the process through which a society moves to acquire capability of enhancing the quality of life of the people, primarily through the solution of its economic problems or increasing the per capita income.

But the analysis also shows that more than the role of the television the role of the developmental agencies assume higher responsibilities and value in the appropriate utilization of television for rural development. An analysis of developmental agencies provided the understanding of the dynamics of rural elites who manipulate it in such a way that the fruits of developmental programmes could be pocketed by a few like the Mukhia of Ismailpur. The location of the television and its "free" access to everyone helped in breaking the communication barrier related to development. But, due to an impervious infrastructure, very little could be achieved even after the availability of information. As and when the infrastructure support was provided, adoption of innovations by various categories of cultivators was possible. Otherwise, only the rich could take advantage as it was happening prior to the arrival of the television. The positive contribution of the television in providing information was in those areas where it suggested 'do-it-yourself' kind of ideas. Such ideas were not dependent upon the mercies of developmental agencies and at the same time were within the means of the adopters.

The analysis presented so far, provide a differential perception of the viewers according to their socio-economic status in the village. For landless labourers, the moving pictures were like fairy tales, not helping towards a better living. They remained high sounding ideas without any practical consequence. For the small cultivators in the village, most of the agricultural practices and innovations were capital intensive, meant for rich and large cultivators. For them it was state of helplessness in which the new knowledge could not be used due to a lack of required finances and support from the developmental agencies. The opinion of rich cultivators was characteristically opposite to this view. They viewed television as an instrument of instigation of the poor against the rich. They saw the television message as an evil force for destroying the existing *status quo* and the so-called harmony of the village. In a nutshell nobody seemed to be satisfied.

It would be an interesting research area to investigate whether such an impasse would lead to maintenance of the *statns quo* or create a condition for mobilising forces of change thereby leading to desirable change towards an egalitarian system in rural India.

The methodological contribution of the present study lies in providing process analysis of communication and its eventual effects. As this study is limited to a single village, it may not be possible to generalise the finding of this study for the entire North Bihar but the process analysis undoubtedly helps in the understanding of the broader features of the stages of a message before its adoption or rejection. Further analysis on similar lines would help in contributing the theories of human communication and the role of mass media in rural development and education because whatever the information may be by any medium it has to pass through the human channel.

APPENDIX-A

The 20-points of the Economic Programme are as following :

1. Continuance of steps to bring down prices of essential commodities. Streamlined production, procurement and distribution of essential commodities. Strict economy in government expenditure.
2. Implementation of agricultural land ceiling and speedier distribution of surplus land and compilation of land records.
3. Stepping up of provision of house-sites for landless and weaker section.
4. Bonded labour, wherever it exists, will be declared illegal.
5. Plan for liquidation of rural indebtedness. Legislation for moratorium on recovery of debt from landless labourers, small farmers and artisans.
6. Review of laws on minimum agricultural wages.
7. Five million more hectares to be brought under irrigation. National programme for use of underground water.
8. An accelerated power programme. Super thermal stations under central control.
9. New development plant for development of handloom sector.
10. Improvement in quality and supply of people's cloth.
11. Socialisation of urban and urbanisable land. Ceiling on ownership and possession of vacant land on plinth area of new dwelling units.
12. Special squads for valuation of conspicuous consumption and prevention of tax evasion. Summary trials and deterrent punishment for economic offenders.
13. Special legislation for confiscation of smuggler's properties.
14. Liberalization of investment procedures. Action against misuse of import licences.
15. New schemes for workers' association in industry.
16. National permit scheme for road transport.
17. Income tax relief to middle class—exemption limit raised to Rs. 8,000.

18. Essential commodities at controlled prices to students in hostels.
19. Books and stationery at controlled prices.
20. New apprenticeship scheme to enlarge employment and training, especially of weaker sections.

BIBLIOGRAPHICAL REFERENCES

Adivi Reddy, A. (1980). "What Ails our Rural Communication" ? In *Rural Development and Communication Policies*. New Delhi : Indian Institute of Mass Communication, pp. 54-58.

Aghi, Mira B. (1977). *Impact of Science Education Programme on SITE Children of Rajasthan*. Ahmedabad : Space Applications Centre.

Agrawal, Binod C. (1978). *Television Comes to Village : An Evaluation of SITE*. Bangalore : Indian Space Research Organisation.

Agrawal, Binod C. (1981). *SITE Social Evaluation : Results, Experiences and Implications*. Ahmedabad : Space Applications Centre.

Alexander, F.D. *et al.* (1963). "A Field Experiment in Diffusion of Knowledge of Diary Cattle Feeding through a TV School". *Rural Sociology*, Vol. 28(2), pp. 400-404.

Bates, Tony and John Robinson (eds.) (1977). *Evaluating Educational Television and Radio*. Milton Keynes : The Open University Press.

Belson, Willium (1977). Television Violence and the Adolesent Boys. *Intermedia*, Vol. 5(6), pp. 20-24.

Beltran, S.L.R. (1976). Alien Premises, Objectives and Methods in Latin American Communication Research. *Communication Research*, Vol. 3(2).

Berelson, Bernard (1952). "Content Analysis in Communication Research." *Reader in Public Opinion and Communication* (second edition). Berelson and Janowitz, (eds.) New York : The Free Press, pp. 260-266.

Bhaskaran, P. assisted by Ila Patel (1977). *SITE for Children : Morning Feedback*. Ahmedabad : Space Applications Centre.

Bhatia, B.S. (1977). *SITE-TV Set Performance*. Ahmedabad : Space Applications Centre.

Black, James and Dean J. Champion (1976). *Methods and Issues in Social Research*. New York : John Wiley & Sons, Inc.,

Blalock, Hubert M. (Jr.) (1970). *An Introduction to Social Research*. New Jarsey : Prentice-Hall, Inc.,

Blumer, Herbert (1969). *Symbolic Interactionism--Perspective and Method.* New Jersey : Prentice-Hall, Inc..

Bogart, Leo (1966). "Audiences." In *National Educational Television and Radio Centre : A Fact Book.* New York : The Centre.

Borra, Ranjan (1970). "Communication through Television : UNESCO Adult Education Experiments in France Japan, and India". *Journal of Communication,* Vol. 20(1).

Brooks, W.D. (1971). *Speech Communication,* Dubugue, Iowa : William C. Brown Publishers.

Chauhan, K.N.K. and B.P. Sinha (1976). "Impact of SITE on Adoption of Farm Technology". *Indian Journal of Extention Education,* Vol. XIII (3 & 4), pp. 14-21.

Chauhan, K.N.K. and B.P. Sinha (1977). "Effects of SITE TV on Democratic—Conservative Outlook of the Rural Audience". *Indian Journal of Extention Education,* Vol. XIII (1 & 2), pp. 9-14.

Chauhan, K.N.K. and B.P. Sinha (1979). "Impact of SITE Television on the Audiences' Efficacy and Faith in Norms." *Indian Journal of Extention Education,* Vol. XV (3 & 4), pp. 15-21.

Chitnis, E.V. (1976). "Introduction to SITE". In *SITE Winter School,* January 16-28, 1976. Ahmedabad : Space Applications Centre. pp. 5-16.

Coldevin, Gary O. (1977). "Television Effects on Canadian Arctic High School Students : A Cross-cultural Comparison." *Evaluating Educational Television and Radio.* Bates and Robinson, (eds.) Milton Keynes : The Open University Press, pp. 61-64.

Dale, E. (1963). *Audio-Visual Methods in Teaching.* New York : Holt, Rinehart and Winston.

Damle, Y.C. (1959). "Harikatha—A Study in Communication". In *S.K. De Felicitation Volume.* Poona : Bulletin of Deccan College Research Institute.

Dey, P.K. (1968). "Relative Effectiveness of Radio and Television as Mass Communication Media in Dissemination of Agricultural Information." Unpublished M. Sc. Thesis. New Delhi : Indian Agricultural Research Institute.

Dube, S.C. (1976). "Development Change and Communication in India." In *Communication and Change : The Last Ten Years—and the Next.* Schramm and Lerner, (eds.) Honolulu : The East West Centre, pp. 98-118.

Eapen, K.E. *et al.* (1979). "Evaluation of Karnataka SITE Experience." *'SITE Studies'—a Critical Assessment of the Studies Relating to the SITE*. Compiled by M.S. Gore, Bombay : Tata Institute of Social Sciences, pp. 322-330.

Firth, Raymond (1973). *Symbols Public and Private*. London : George Allen & Unwin Ltd.

Fischer, J.L. (1973). "Communication in Primitive Systems". *Handbook of Communication*. Pool and Frey, (eds.) Chicago : Rand McNally College Publishing Company, pp. 313-336.

Forcess, D.P. and Stephen Richer (1973). *Social Research Methods*. New Jersey, Prentice-Hall, Inc..

Foster, G.M. (1962). *Traditional Cultures and Impact of Technological Changes*. New York : Harper & Row Publisher.

Gaikwad, V.R. *et al.* (1973). *Rural Social Structure and Communication in an Indian Village*. Ahmedabad : Indian Institute of Management.

Gokhale, L.N. (1973). "TV as a Supporting Medium". In *Material on Development Communication*, Special Course (September 3-29, 1979), Pune : Film and Television Institute of India, pp. 51-56.

Gore, M.S. (1979). *A Critical Assessment of the Studies relating to the SITE*. Bombay : Tata Institute of Social Sciences.

Gross, Bertram M. (1973). "Introduction of the New Field of Urban Communication Part (IV)." *Communication Technology and Social Policy*. Gerbner, Gross, and Melody, (eds.) New York : John Wiley & Sons, pp. 289-292.

Gumperz, J.J. and Hymes, D.M. (eds.) (1964). "Ethnography of Communication." *American Anthropologist*, Vol. 66 (6-11), pp. i-iv. (special publication).

Hach, M.T.V. (1967). "The Forms of Organizing of the Introduction of Progressive and Practical Experience and Scientific and Technological Results in Agricultural Production of Czechoslovakia." *Journal of Institute for Scientific and Technical Information*, Vol. 16(1).

Halls, Edward T. (1959). *The Salient Language*, Paperback edition. New York : Garden City Doubleday.

Harris, Marvin (1968). *The Rice of Anthropological Theory*. New York : Thomas Y. Crowell Company.

Harrison, Gordon Scott (1972). "Flow of Communication between Government Agencies and Eskimo Village." *Human Organization*, Vol. 31(1), pp. 3-5.

Hein, Norvin (1959). "The Ramlila." In *Traditional Media : Structure and Change*. Milton Singer, (ed.) *Journal of American Folklore*, Vol. 71 (special volume), pp. 279-304.

Hitchcock, J.T. and Leigh Minturn (1963). "The Rajputs of Khalapur, India". *Six Cultures : Studies of Child Rearing.* Beatrice B. Whiting, (ed.) New York : John Wiley and Sons, Inc. pp. 207-361.

Kearl, Bryant E. (1976). "Communication for Agriculture Development." In *Communication and Change : The Last Ten Years - and the Next.* Schramm and Lerner, (eds.) Honolulu : The East-West Center, pp. 163-183.

Kluckhohn, Clyde (1961). "Notes on some Anthropological Aspects of Communication." *American Anthropologist*, Vol. 63(5-1), pp. 859-910.

Lakshman Rao, Y.V. (1966). *Communication and Development : A Study of Two Indian Villages.* Minneapolis : University of Minnesota Press.

Lazarsfeld, P.F. and Merton R.K. (1971). "Mass Communication, Popular Teste, and Organised Social Action". In *The Process and Effects of Mass Communication.* Schramm and Roberts, (eds.) Urbana : University of Illinois Press, pp. 554-578.

Lesser, Gerald S. (1974). *Children and Television : Lessons from CTW Sesame Street.* New York : Random House Inc.

Lionberger, H.F. (1958). "Television Viewing in Rural Borne Country with special reference to Agricultural shows." *Bulletin No. 702.* Missouri : Agricultural Experiment Station.

Liu, Alan P.L. (1971). *Communication and National Integration in Communist China.* Bombay : Oxford University Press.

Maccoby, Eleanor E. (1963). "The Effects of Television on Children". In *The Science of Human Communication*, Wilbur Schramm, (ed.) New York : Basic Books.

Maccoby, Eleanor E. (1969). "Early Stimulation and Cognitive Development." In *Minnesota Symposium on Child Psychology.* J.P. Hill, (ed.) Minneapolis : University of Minnesota Press.

Majumdar, D.N. (1958). *Caste and Communication in an Indian Village.* Bombay : Asia Publishing House.

Marriott, McKim (1960). *Caste Ranking and Community Structure in Five Regions of India and Pakistan.* Poona : G.S. Press.

McCormack, William (1959). "Forms of Communication in Viashaiva Religion". "Traditional India : Structure and Change." *Journal of American Folklore*, Vol. 71 (special volume), pp. 119-125.

McQuail, Devis (1977). "The Influence and Effects of Mass Media." In *Mass Communication and Society.* Curran, Gurevitch, and Woolacott, (eds.) London : The Open University Press, pp. 71-94.

Mishra, A.N. (1967). "Impact of Television on Farmers." Unpublished M.Sc. Thesis. New Delhi : Indian Agricultural Research Institute.

Mody, Bella with Dalpat Sarupriya (1977). *SITE Message Systems Analysis-What did SITE Programmes Consist of?* Ahmedabad : Space Applications Centre.

Montague, Ashley (1967). *The Human Dialogue.* New York : The Free Press.

Nascimento, Kit (1977). Using Communication to Support Development : Guyanan. In *Issues in Communications,* No. 1, London : International Institute of Communications, pp. 16-20.

National Council of Educational Research and Training (1968). *Impact of Agricultural Television Programme on Farmers in Delhi.* New Delhi, DAE/NCERT.

Pal, Yash (1977). "Space Projects for Developing Countries." Paper presenting in the meeting of the UN Committee on the Peaceful Uses of Outer Space, held at Vienna, June 20—July 1, 1977.

Pool, Ithiel De Sola (1973). "Communication in Totalitarian Societies." *Handbook of Communication.* Pool and F. Frey. (eds.) Chicago : Rand McNally College Publishing Company, pp. 462-511.

Rogers, E.M. (1962). *Diffusion of Innovations,* New York : The Free Press.

Rudolph L'loyd and Susanne H. Rudolph (1960). "Opinion Survey in India." In *Reader in Public Opinion and Communication.* Berelson and Janowitz, (eds.) New York : The Free Press (second edition), pp. 745-755.

Sachchidananda (1972). *Social Dimension of Agricultural Development.* Delhi : National Publishing House.

Sachchidananda and M.N. Jha (1980). *Communication in a Bihar Village : An Evaluation of SITE,* Ahmedabad : Space Applications Centre.

Sanga, G.S. *et al.* (1979). "Awareness of the Rural TV Viewers about the Development Programmes of Amritsar Doordarshan." *Journal of Extension Education,* Vol. XV(3 & 4), pp. 74-76.

Sankariah, Ch. (1969). "A Study of Differential Communication Patterns in a Progressive and a Non-Progressive village." Unpublished Ph.D. Thesis. New Delhi : Indian Agricultural Research Institute.

Sarabhai, Vikram A. (1969). "Television for Development." Paper presented in the Society for International Development Conferences, New Delhi.

Schramm, Wilbur (1964). *Mass Media and National Development.* California : Stanford University Press.

Searle, Ann (1977). "Children's Perception and Understanding of Television." In *Evaluating Educational Television and Radio.* Bates and Robinson, (eds.) Milton Keynes : The Open University Press, pp. 101-102.

Sekhon, Indrajit (1968). "A Pilot Study to assess the Effectiveness of Television as a Medium of Communication for Imparting Technical Know-how to the Farmers." Unpublished MSc. Thesis. New Delhi : Lady Irwin College.

Sharma, S.K. and Jagadish Singh (1972). *Television in Agricultural Transformation.* New Delhi : Indian Council of Agricultural Research.

Shroff, A.A. (1976). "SITE : Software Aspect." In *SITE Winter School,* January 16-28, Ahmedabad : Space Applications Centre, pp. 83-96.

Shukla, Snehlata and Kuldip Kumar (1977). *SITE Impact Study on Children.* Ahmedabad : Space Applications Centre.

Shummo, Ali (1977). "Delivering Social Services in Sudan. *Issues in Communications,* No. 1, London : International Institute of Communications, pp. 27-29.

Singhi, P.M. *et al.* "Village Affluence, Knowledge Gap, and Satellite Television." *CMA Monograph* No. 82, Ahmedabad : Indian Institute of Management.

Sinha, B.P. (1974). *Television in Diffusion of Farm Information.* Delhi : New Heights.

Verghese, B.G. (1980). "A Philosophy for Development Communication : The View from India." In *Television for Education and Development.* B.S. Bhatia, (ed.) Ahmedabad : Space Applications Centre, pp. 1-24.

Wallace, Anthony F.C. (1970). *Culture and Personality,* New York : Random House (second edition).

INDEX